P9-ECZ-674

Researching
Social Processes
in the Laboratory

CONTEMPORARY STUDIES IN SOCIOLOGY, VOLUME 6

Editor: John Clark, *Department of Sociology, University of Minnesota*

CONTEMPORARY STUDIES IN SOCIOLOGY

Theoretical and Empirical Monographs

Editor: John Clark
Department of Sociology, University of Minnesota

Volume 1. **THE ENTREPRENEURIAL BUREAUCRACY: BIOGRAPHIES OF TWO FEDERAL PROGRAMS IN EDUCATION**
Ronald G. Corwin, Department of Sociology,
Ohio State University

Volume 2. **TRANSITION TO THE 21ST CENTURY: PROSPECTS AND POLICIES FOR ECONOMIC AND URBAN-REGIONAL TRANSFORMATION**
Edited by Donald A. Hicks, School of Social Sciences, University of Texas at Dallas, and Norman J. Glickman, Department of City and Regional Planning and Regional Science, University of Pennsylvania

Volume 3. **ORGANIZATIONS AND THEIR ENVIRONMENTS: ESSAYS IN THE SOCIOLOGY OF ORGANIZATIONS**
Charles K. Warriner, Department of Sociology,
University of Kansas

Volume 4. **INTERDISCIPLINARY THEORIES OF RURAL DEVELOPMENT**
Frank W. Young, Department of Rural Sociology,
Cornell University

Volume 5. **CONSTRUCTING CIVILIZATIONS**
Carl J. Couch, Department of Sociology,
University of Iowa

Volume 6. **RESEARCHING SOCIAL PROCESSES IN THE LABORATORY**
Carl J. Couch, Department of Sociology,
University of Iowa

Researching Social Processes in the Laboratory

by CARL J. COUCH
Department of Sociology
University of Iowa

JAI PRESS INC.

Greenwich, Connecticut *London, England*

Library of Congress-in-Catalog'ing-in-Publication Data
Couch, Carl J.
Researching social processes in the laboratory.

(Contemporary studies in sociology ; v. 6)
Bibliography: p.
Includes indexes.
1. Sociology—Research—Methodology. 2. Small groups
—Research—Methodology. I. Title. II. Series.
HM48.C68 1987 301′.072 87-2758
ISBN 0-89232-823-1

55 Old Post Road, No. 2
Greenwich, Connecticut 06836

JAI PRESS LTD.
3 Henrietta Street
London WC2E 8LU
England

ISBN: 0-89232-823-1
Library of Congress Catalog Card Number: 87-2758
Manufactured in the United States of America

CONTENTS

List of Diagrams

Preface

Early in my career I became disenchanted with the methodologies that dominated sociology. I concluded that neither survey research nor naturalistic observation generated the data necessary for the formulation of viable principles of social life. I took it as an article of faith that principles of social life were possible and was convinced that if any such principles were to be formulated they would be generated from the sustained and systematic analyses of social phenomena. I remain convinced that such principles cannot be derived by logic, intuition, nor other forms of arm-chair theorizing.

Experiences derived from two major research undertakings, one a study of a protest group and the other a study of problem drinkers, convinced me that an adequate explanation of human action required the close and systematic study of social processes. Both studies were based on a combination of survey data and field observations. But, neither questionnaire responses nor the field notes generated data adequate to answer the questions. It became apparent that the acquisition of adequate data required close observation of social interaction.

The small groups laboratory tradition appeared to provide procedures for making close observations of social interaction. However the laboratory research of sociologists conducted during the 1960s and 1970s had become very nonsociological. The guidelines provided by Bales (1950) and others focus on the individual acting within a social context; they do not focus on social acts. Furthermore, as anyone who has attempted to make observations of social phenomena in the laboratory knows, it is very difficult for an observer or even a team of observers of social phenomena to make anything approaching a comprehensive record of the social events produced by pluralities of interacting individuals. It is even more difficult to achieve satisfactory levels of interobserver reliability.

The emerging video technology caught my attention. I thought it might offer a solution to some of the observational problems associated with the study of interaction processes. A vague program of research that combined the controls of the laboratory with video technology to enhance observations was formulated. Howard Erhlich, Steve Spitzer, and I were successful in enticing the University of Iowa to establish a small groups laboratory equipped with video recording units—The Center for Research on Interpersonal Behavior (CRIB).

When I first began conducting research of social processes in CRIB there were no viable guidelines for combining the laboratory and video recording technology with the sociological tradition. The laboratory research that was being conducted by sociologists was, for all practical purposes, nonsociological. A few social scientists were making audio recorders of conversations, but almost no social scientists were making audio-visual recordings of social events. And, of the few who were making recordings none had combined the technology with laboratory controls.

Many mistakes were made. I knew nothing about how to manage the equipment, very little about how to elicit specimens of social action within the laboratory, and even less about how to analyze recordings of social action. For the first few years the data generated and recorded were essentially worthless. Time, money, and energy were wasted. Sufficient expertise in the management of the equipment was acquired easily. It took somewhat longer to develop skill in creating contexts within the laboratory that elicited select specimens of social action and considerably longer for the expertise to analyze recordings of social action to emerge. By the early 1970s we had learned to manage the equipment effectively, how to elicit selected specimens of social processes in the laboratory, and a modicum of expertise in analyzing the recordings had emerged.

We achieved our first success in 1974 when the elements of

sociation that constitute cooperative action were isolated (Miller, Hintz, and Couch, 1975). Specimens of social action elicited in the laboratory and recorded on video tape provided the data base for the accomplishment. But, more than that was involved. We had also learned to maintain a sociological standpoint when analyzing the data. That was the most significant methodological accomplishment. In retrospect the difficulty of that achievement seems ludicrous. After all at the heart of the sociological tradition is the article of faith that social phenomena have a sui generis standing. However, whereas the sociological tradition has called for the study of social phenomena when sociologists have mounted empirical efforts more often than not they have attended to nominal objectifications of characteristics of individuals and groups (Travisano, 1975: 263), not to social processes. The empirical study of social processes requires making the dyad—two individuals capable of independent action who are acting interdependently—the unit of analysis. That simple but profound dictum became one of the foundation stones of our research.

I offer this set of guidelines for researching social processes in the hope that it will contribute to the development of a more viable social science. Perhaps by using these guidelines others interested in researching social processes in the laboratory will make fewer mistakes than I did. I also hope that it will entice some of my fellow social scientists who are committed to the belief that human life only exists in process, but who have their doubts about the viability of laboratory research to give serious consideration to laboratory research. Social processes can be studied in the laboratory as well as in the field.

Conversations with friends and acquaintances, especially those who subscribe to a processual ontology, have convinced me that many eschew the laboratory and video technology because of their uncertainty on how to proceed. I well remember my own uncertainty, awe, and confusion when I first embarked on this type of research. Others reject it from their conviction that the use of the laboratory necessarily requires adoption of a positivistic ontology. Such is not the case. Perhaps this statement will convince some of those who reject positivism that they can use the laboratory without becoming positivists.

If the guidelines are followed it is relatively easy to acquire the expertise necessary to research social processes and social relationships in the laboratory. The expertise necessary to manage the recording equipment can be acquired in an afternoon. The expertise necessary to create an ecology in the laboratory that will allow for eliciting specimens of social action can be acquired almost as easily. It is somewhat more difficult to acquire the expertise necessary for creating social contexts in the laboratory that will elicit select forms of social processes and relationships. That expertise is acquired by merging a sociological imagination with the laboratory and the recording technology. Far too many sociologists have checked their sociological imaginations at the door when they have entered the laboratory. The effective use of the laboratory and recording equipment for sociological purposes requires that sociologists subordinate the laboratory and the recording equipment to their sociological imaginations, not the reverse as has often been the case. Advanced undergraduates and beginning graduate students can become adept at creating contexts in the laboratory that generate useful data in a few weeks. It probably takes established sociologists slightly longer.

The most difficult set of procedures to master is the intricacies of a sociological analysis of the data. Most advanced undergraduates and beginning graduate students can master the rudimentary analytic procedures of a sociological analysis of recorded specimens of social action in a semester. Again, it probably is more difficult for established sociologists to acquire the skill.

Most of the illustrations offered are taken from studies completed in CRIB. The illustrations reflect the interests of those associated with CRIB. Many of the studies focused on various aspects of negotiating. However, the procedures can be applied to a host of other sociological issues. They have been applied to studies of accounting, bargaining, authority relationships, triadic structures, diffusion and socialization. They can be effectively employed to study identity transformation, alienation, anomie, exploitation, social change, and social mobility.

Only a few arguments justifying the epistemology are offered. More extended rationales for the methodology can be found in *Constructing Social Life,* (Couch and Hintz, 1975) and *Studies in Symbolic Interaction: The Iowa School,* (Couch, Saxton, and Katovich, 1986). This statement is primarily a "how to do it" manual; it is not a treatize on epistemology. Similarly, this statement does not report the results of studies, but how the results were achieved.

Many contributed to the development of these procedures. In fact the contributions of others are so extensive it is somewhat presumptuous of me to offer them under my name. In the early stumbling years, Frank Kohout, Stan Saxton, Mark Wardell, Richard Bord, and Steven Norland made major contributions to the merger of the sociological imagination with the laboratory and recording technology. Later, Dan Miller, Robert Hintz, Marilyn Leichty, Glenda Sehested, Marion Weiland, Steven Buban, and Ron Neff refined the merger. They were primarily responsible for the development of procedures for the sociological analysis of the data. Subsequently others have elaborated, refined, and extended the procedures. They include Stu Stover, Mike Katovich, Barbara Sink, Nawal Lutfyyia, Monica Hardesty, Joel Powell, and Mari Molseed.

The biases of each medium of communication sometimes make it difficult to translate ideas developed in one medium into another. Video recordings display information as a moving gestalt; writing displays information in static form. Many of the ideas contained in this statement emerged from transactions between researchers and an electronic medium—television. It has occasionally been difficult to put these ideas into writing. Reciprocally, those who read this statement and attempt to implement the procedures may experience some moments of frustration. Two instructional video tapes are available that might alleviate some to the difficulty. One is entitled *The Study of Social Processes I: Design*, the other, *The Study of Social Processes II: Analysis.*[1] The first offers a step-by-step procedure for establishing laboratory contexts that will elicit three types of social action—interpersonal negotiations, authority relationships, and intergroup negotiations. The second offers some suggestions for how to complete analyses of video recordings of social encounters. They present some of the ideas in the original medium.

Finally, a special note of thanks to Stan Saxton for his many insightful comments on an earlier draft.

NOTE

1. Both video tape are available from the Video Center, The University of Iowa, Iowa city, Iowa 52242.

Chapter I

The Promise

Social scientists generate and analyze data in many different ways. Data generating procedures range from the administration of questionnaires, spying, searching through bureaucratic files, living with those the object of investigation, viewing persons in a small groups laboratory through one-way mirrors, digging up artifacts deposited by ancient groups, and recording social transactions. Procedures for data analysis are also highly varied. They include descriptive statistical summaries, correlations, analytical induction, qualitative analysis, and interpretative analysis (Denzin, 1978).

Whatever the methods of data generation and analysis all social science researchers presume that the acquisition and examination of data contribute to understanding social life. Most social scientists presume that a science of social life is possible. Some critics question the possibility of a science of social life—the ability of social scientists to formulate valid abstract assertions about social phenomena. These critics marshal many arguments in support of their position. One of them is that the tremendous complexity and variability of social life makes a science of social life an impossibility.

Those social scientists who believe a science of social life is possible explicitly reject this argument. They presume that valid abstract propositions about social life can be formulated on the basis of the acquisition and analysis of data. Those social scientists who believe in the possibility of sociology becoming an empirical science agree that one may make statements about social life without linking the characterizations to data. But, they take the position that the validity of assertions can be demonstrated only by displaying data which justify the propositions offered (Schwartz and Jacobs, 1979: 3).

The arguments among social science researchers is not about the relevance or significance of empirical phenomena, but over what data are the most useful and what procedures of data analysis are the most powerful. Those who administer questionnaires and make statistical analyses of questionnaire responses presume that questionnaire responses provide the necessary artifacts for constructing a science of social life. They further presume that statistics offer the most efficacious procedure for the analysis of data. Those who acquire data through naturalistic observation and follow the dictates of analytic induction disagree. They think naturalistic observations have greater validity than questionnaire responses. Most advocates of naturalistic observation regard analytic induction as superior to statistics for the analysis of data.

THE LABORATORY

The laboratory has a long tradition in social sciences. Over 50 years ago Sherif (1935) employed laboratory procedures to study the formation of social norms; also, in the 1930s Lewin and his associates completed laboratory studies of group structures (Lewin, Lippet, and White, 1939); somewhat later Asch (1951) completed laboratory studies of social pressure and conformity. These researchers used the laboratory to create conditions that focused attention on phenomena that they judged critical for the formulation of more complete and accurate characterizations of some dimensions of social life. They used the laboratory to examine select phenomena in "pure" form. They created conditions that excluded many extraneous factors so that they might observe the critical phenomena in purer form. They used the laboratory to generate uncluttered specimens of social action.

The laboratory setting is a paradox. On the one hand, the intention of laboratory researchers is to create conditions that will allow for the observation of what otherwise is not or might not be observable. On the other hand, in the process of bringing the phenomena of interest to the laboratory there is always the risk of destroying the phenomena or so mangling them that they are no longer recognizable. Many sociologists who have attempted laboratory research have created contexts within the laboratory that have made it impossible for the phenomena of interest to sociologists—social processes and relationships—to appear. For example, the research tradition informed by expectation states theory conducts laboratory studies, but those researchers do not elicit social phenomena in the laboratory (Berger and Zelditch, 1985). Needless to say, while such studies may provide us with knowledge of how individuals respond to various situations, do not generate the data necessary to acquire greater understanding of social processes. At the absolute minimum, if greater understandings of social processes are to be acquired from laboratory research it is necessary to generate social processes—people acting with, toward, for, and against each other—in the laboratory. The processes of observation always influence what is observed, but laboratory manipulations often transform, and even sometimes destroy, the phenomena of interest. Those social scientists who use the laboratory to elicit specimens of social action have to be very sensitive to the relationships between themselves and their subjects if they are to elicit sociological data in the laboratory. The generation of units of social action within the laboratory "requires an imagination that does justice to the everyday world of human affairs, but at the same time magnifies selected features of social life" (Katovich, 1984: 55). That requires making the actions of dyads, not a series of individuals, the target of observation.

Unfortunately, when some social scientists have used the laboratory they have followed the guidelines of their psychological brethren and created contexts that exposed individuals to various stimuli and noted the reactions of persons to the stimuli. Often the participants in laboratory studies have not been allowed to interact, but only to respond to stimuli provided by the experimenter. The phenomena of concern for sociologists is not the activity of individuals or even the activity of aggregates of individuals. The objects of investigation for social scientists are social activities.

If social scientists are to make effective use of the laboratory they must create social contexts and then entice a plurality of persons to interact within social contexts. The minimum unit of observation for social scientists is two or more persons acting with each other to achieve one or more social objective. When properly used, the laboratory is a provocative stage that elicits vibrant social processes.

Some studies of social phenomena have generated social processes in the laboratory, but failed to maintain a sociological standpoint when analyzing the data. For example, in the early studies of Bales (1950), persons were enticed to interact in a laboratory context, but he analyzed his data by noting the frequency of different acts performed by individuals. But the mere counting of individual acts does not constitute a sociological analysis. To complete a sociological analysis it is necessary to note what *they*—a plurality of individuals—do. Social acts, not personal acts, are the focus of concern for social scientists.

The laboratory, when properly used, makes two major contributions. One, it provides the means for "highlighting" the phenomena under investigation. Well designed laboratory studies provide a context wherein relatively pure specimens of a given form of social activity are elicited. The social activity in question is thereby more amenable to detailed examination, and two, the laboratory minimizes interferences from extraneous factors. The removal of extraneous factors facilitates the systematic examination of those events deemed critical for acquiring greater understanding of phenomena under examination.

By convening persons in a laboratory and carefully specifying a context it is possible to elicit units of social action in relatively pure form. However, even then the researcher is still confronted by exceedingly complex phenomena. Human beings simultaneously respond and initiate; they simultaneously communicate in discourse (Mead, 1934), appearance (Stone, 1962), and touch (Leichty, 1975). No one is capable of making all of the observations necessary to acquire anything approaching a complete record of what transpires in even simple interactional sequences of short duration. By combining the small group laboratory with video recording technology it is possible to obtain a much more complete record of social encounters than when unaided observations are made.

VIDEO RECORDINGS

Many technological devices have been used to extend the observational acuity of researchers in other fields of study. It was the telescope that allowed Galileo to observe the moons of Jupiter and thereby acquire additional data in support of the Copernican theory of planetary movement. The telescope revolutionized astronomy (Wolf, 1950). It was not welcomed with open arms by all astronomers. A few of the doubting Thomases of the day believed that the observations displayed by the telescope were merely artifacts of the telescope; that somehow there was something in the telescope that made it appear that there were moons circling Jupiter.

In a similar manner the microscope provided the means for observing previously unobservable microorganisms. The usefulness of the microscope was not immediately recognized by biologists (Mayr, 1982). The microorganisms revealed by the microscope were the topic of conversation among intellectual dilettantes for many years before biologists gave them serious consideration. Microscopic observations eventually provided the empirical foundation for disease theory; and, of course, in due time microscopes became the instruments of observation for organic scientists just as telescopes became the instruments of observation for astronomers.

The telescope and microscope are extensions of the human sensorium (McLuhan, 1962). They have allowed human beings to make observations of inorganic and organic phenomena that were previously not possible. They provided new and more precise data. These devices allowed researchers to generate data that led to the formulation of new concepts and theories. The detection of additional phenomena, the development of new concepts and the formulation of new propositions modified and transformed established explanations. The new theories provided more comprehensive and integrated accounts of phenomena and allowed researchers to explore new arenas.

In a similar manner, audio-visual recording technologies provide social scientists with the opportunity to make more complete and refined observations of social processes than can be made by unaided observers. And, they provide observational procedures that are superior to questionnaires where the respondents are asked to report on their experiences and action to researchers. Audio-visual recording technologies allow for the accumulation of new types of data. They promise a partial solution to the observational problems of sociologists. The data provided by recordings can be brought to bear on old questions and new questions can be posed. These recordings, if properly made, provide data of high fidelity that are researchable and shareable (Couch, 1986a). These devices provide a means for partially overcoming the obstacles that are posed by the fact that sociological researchers have to confront complex and ever moving phenomena if they are to formulate principles of social action.

Whereas the telescope and microscope allowed human beings to observe phenomena not previously observable, video recordings do not expose phenomena to observation that were not previously observable. Rather, they allow for more accurate and precise observations than are possible by unaided human observation. Furthermore, the data are far more retrievable than are data stored in human memory supplemented by field notes.

The replay and slow motion features of recordings allow for the sustained, systematic, and public examination of visual and auditory displays of social activities. Recordings thereby also provide a partial solution to the difficulties of achieving interobserver reliability of social phenomena. When unaided observations are made of social events it is a common occurrence for two persons who have witnessed the events to disagree about what occurred. Audio-visual recordings are widely used for this purpose. Sports commentators, directors of entertainment productions, athletic coaches, and biological scientists use the technology to sharpen their observations. However, social scientists have made only limited use of television recordings in their studies of social phenomena. Fewer still have combined video recordings with laboratory research.

Some social scientists have used recording devices to record "naturally occurring events." Conversations have been recorded and researched by a number of social scientists (Schegloff, 1968; Jefferson, 1972; Lennard and Bernstein 1969; Mead and Bateson, 1977; Mishler and Waxler, 1968; and Schegloff and Sacks,

1973). Their experience suggests that the effective use of recording technology requires that researchers exercise great control in the selection of phenomena to be recorded. Recordings provide such a wealth of data that researchers often are overwhelmed by the data. To effectively use the technology for the study of social processes it is necessary to be very selective when making recordings.

AN EXAMPLE

Video recordings of two preselected sets of specimens of social action generated within a laboratory provided the data that allowed for the isolation of the elements of sociation that constitute cooperative action and the structure of those elements (Miller, Hintz, and Couch, 1975). The central question addressed in the early stages of that research undertaking was: How is coordinated action achieved? That general question was derived from the theoretical statements of Mead (1934) and Blumer (1969) and further specified by Kuhn's (1962) and Miyamoto's (1970) statements on the nature of the social act. Some of the implications of these statements and Schegloff's (1968) research on openings, which was based on audio recordings, provided the general framework for organizing a research effort to isolate the elements of sociation that compose coordinated action.

A situation was created in the laboratory wherein video recordings were made of two persons who were co-present but acting independently of each other. Specifically, two sets of dyads, one-half strangers and the other half friends, were convened in the laboratory. Each member of each dyad was asked to independently complete a questionnaire. After they had begun filling out their questionnaires a recording of a staged accident was played in the next room. The actions of each dyad were recorded.

In brief, a laboratory context was created to elicit the construction of social openings from two different sets of dyads. The activities produced by these dyads when moving from acting independently to acting interdependently were video taped. These recordings were subsequently analyzed to isolate the joint activities that constitute the construction of a social opening.

Given the fact that we rather constantly construct openings a reasonable question is: Why study openings in the laboratory? A second reasonable question is: Why record such elementary units of social action?

The primary reason for conducting laboratory studies of any phenomena is to reduce clutter. Social openings, and all other units of coordinated action, constructed in uncontrolled situations are produced within a tremendously wide variety of contexts and in response to an equally wide variety of events. By eliciting openings within a standardized situation uncontaminated by extraneous factors it was possible to remove much of the clutter. Consequently, the basic elements of sociation that constitute openings were more easily detected. It is very doubtful that the elements of sociation that compose openings to coordinated action could have been isolated by the analysis of recordings of openings constructed in uncontrolled situations. At the minimum, such recordings would have contained so much clutter that the analysis of the data would have been far more difficult.

Social openings, especially those constructed by strangers in a laboratory, are a very simple form of social action. Nonetheless, the fact that human beings can respond and initiate simultaneously and can simultaneously communicate via touch, appearance, and discourse frequently makes it almost impossible for even trained observers to reproduce a complete replica of the original actions on the basis of unaided observations. Audio-visual recordings of social acts provide a much more complete replica. Recordings can be "re" "searched"—examined again and again. The notations of trained laboratory and field observers can also be researched. But the data provided by notations, whether by observers or the participants themselves, are far less complete than the data provided by audio-visual recordings (Couch, 1975). The researchability of the recordings facilitated the isolation of the elements of sociation.

When the notations of laboratory of field observers are analyzed the data base consists of the notations plus the memory of the observer. As the analysis proceeds the data base may change when the researchers recall events that were not originally regarded as significant. Consequently the data sets based on unaided observations are far less stable than are the data sets provided by recordings. Researchers nearly always reconceptualize their problem and/or the data while analyzing it. Reconceptualizations often allow the researchers to "see" events previously not noted; and, when the data consist of notations and memories a researcher often recalls events previously ignored. When that occurs, a researcher using notations cannot be certain if the reconceptualization is a more adequate conceptualization of the phenomena under investigation, or merely appears to be a more adequate conceptualization because of his selective recall of events stimulated by his reformulation of the problem and/or the data.

In contrast, when recordings provide the data base as the analysis proceeds, the researcher can be more certain that his reconceptualization is a more adequate one for the data remain constant; the data do not change as a consequence of reconceptualizations. That allows for more sound assessments of the adequacy of reconceptualizations (Couch, 1986a).

Another strength of recordings is that the data are highly shareable. The notations of laboratory and field observers can also be shared, but the degree of shareability is far less. All that can be shared are the notations, not the personal memories. When recordings provide the data base others can listen to and observe the recordings. "Observing and listening to recordings of social activity does not yield the same experiences as on-the-spot observation. Nor do the camera and microphone capture all that is there" (Couch, 1984: 9). But, data sets based on recordings are far more shareable than are data sets based on notations. And, the data are far richer and much more complete than the notations made by laboratory or field observers.

SUMMARY

The laboratory and video recording technology will not solve all the problems of social science researchers. They are only technologies. Even when they are properly used they only provide a partial solution to some of the problems associated with researching social processes. To acquire useful data it is still necessary to use one's sociological imagination (Mills, 1959). A rich and disciplined sociological imagination is far more essential to the completion of a meaningful research enterprise than is either a fancy laboratory or expensive recording equipment. Furthermore, the effective use of these procedures requires that they be subordinated to the sociological tradition and imagination. The sociological tradition and imagination can not be subordinated to the technology. If they are it is a certainty that the technology will not contribute to a greater understanding of social phenomena.

The effective use of the technology requires that units of *social* action be elicited within the laboratory and that the recordings be of *social* action. The generation of data useful to social scientists requires that dyadic interaction, not the behavior of individuals, be recorded. Only by making the dyad the minimal unit of analysis is it possible to make the observations necessary for the formulation of principles of social processes.

One of the objectives of sociological research is to construct new knowledge about social phenomena. That knowledge in turn can then be disseminated so that all will have a more complete understanding of the nature of social life and the consequences of various forms of social life for all. If and as that knowledge is generated, human beings will be able to exercise greater control over their behavior and its consequences.

The laboratory provides the means for spotlighting the phenomena under investigation and controlling for extraneous factors; video technology extends the observational powers of researchers. The two, in combination with a sociological imagination, promise to extend our understanding of social processes. Social scientists are no longer restricted to the generation of static artifacts (questionnaire responses) and unaided (naked ear and eye) observations of social processes. They can now generate and study artifacts that retain the processual qualities of social life. Audio-visual recordings provide data sets of high fidelity. Theories of social life can be modified, refined and elaborated; and, new questions can be asked and answered.

Chapter II

Space and Equipment

The most important dictum to keep in mind when preparing the laboratory and arranging the recording equipment is: Always subordinate the technology to the sociological imagination; never allow the laboratory and equipment to dictate research procedures. The complexity of studies that can be completed is constrained by the space and equipment available. However, a large laboratory and elaborate equipment are not necessary to undertake significant research.

Complex social processes can be generated in one large well-lighted room. The only pieces of equipment absolutely necessary to acquire recordings that are adequate for most analyses are a camera, a microphone, a television monitor, a recording unit, some tapes, and some wiring.

Some researchers made the mistake of being more concerned with the technical quality of the recordings than they are with the sociological quality. The two concerns are not inherently incompatible, but a concern with producing studio-quality recordings can inhibit the generation of high-quality sociological data. If researchers become enamored with the laboratory and recording equipment they are less likely to complete significant research than are those who keep sociological issues in the forefront. An elaborate laboratory layout and expensive equipment only facilitate the generation of high-quality sociological data when they are subordinated to the sociological tradition and used with sociological imagination.

One of the earliest studies completed in CRIB was not as

successful as it might have been because we were more concerned with obtaining recordings of high technical quality than of high sociological quality. The study (Saxton, 1973) was designed to examine how people re-engage in interaction after one of the interactants committed an absurd act. The camera was focused on the target of the disruptive act to obtain high quality recordings of her facial expressions. As a consequence a visual recording of the nonverbal behavior of the person who committed the disruptive act was not acquired. Had the camera been focused on the activities of the dyad instead of one member of the dyad, the data acquired would have been more useful.

Two reasonable rules of thumb are: (1) Use only the minimum amount of space and equipment necessary to generate the date required to address the sociological question at hand, and (2) Always arrange the laboratory and equipment to record the activities of dyads, triads, or larger units.

FURNISHINGS

The term laboratory conjures up the image of a windowless room with sterile white walls housing awe-inspiring equipment. Such a laboratory will inhibit the production of high-quality sociological data. A room or rooms decorated much as a classroom or an office is far more conducive to the acquisition of sound sociological data than is one modelled after biological laboratories. The purpose of biological laboratories is to exclude extraneous factors that interfere with the observation of select specimens of biological phenomena; the purpose of social science laboratories is to exclude extraneous factors that interfere with the generation and observation of uncluttered specimens of social processes and relationships. The two objectives are similar, but the requirements for meeting the two objectives are different.

The target of observation of social scientists is the activities of human beings. An awe-inspiring laboratory is likely to introduce clutter. Such an arrangement will make most volunteers very self-conscious. Most volunteers will be less threatened by a room furnished similar to an office than they will be by one with stark walls filled with elaborate equipment. However, the generation of recordings of high sociological quality requires the exclusion of extraneous sights and sounds. Extraneous sights and sounds distract subjects and they also make transcribing and analyzing the recordings more difficult. Sound proof rooms, or at least rooms removed from heavy foot traffic, are preferable. Similarly, windowless rooms minimize visual distractions. They also make it easier to control the intensity of the lighting so that high-quality visual recordings can be obtained.

Traditionally small groups laboratories have been equipped with one-way mirrors. They provide a means for researchers to observe activities without the researchers being observable or available to the targets of observation. But, with the development of recording technologies they are no longer necessary.

Nearly all volunteers for laboratory studies have heard of social scientists observing subjects through one-way mirrors. Many participants will note the presence of any large mirrors and presume they are being observed by someone on the other side. If the laboratory is equipped with a one-way mirror, cover it with thick curtains or a piece of plywood. Most participants become at least, if not more, self conscious when they know or suspect they are being observed through a one-way mirror than when they know their actions are being recorded.

Concealment of the camera and microphones is counterproductive. It is also of questionable morality. Volunteers know that they are going to be observed. If the camera and microphone are not in plain sight they will attempt to locate them. That can be very distracting. The open placement of the microphone and camera is not more, and probably less, obtrusive than concealment. Furthermore, when the camera and microphones are readily visible it serves as an announcement that at least that dimension of the study is above board. If the volunteers are given a challenging task their task will become their primary focus of attention.

When we recruit subjects they are informed that they will be recorded. At the beginning of each session we state, "As we told you, you will be recorded." The positioner then points to the microphone and camera. The participants are told they may withdraw from the study at any time without penalty and that they will be paid even if they do not complete the session. They are also informed that if after they have completed the session they wish to have the recording erased, we will erase it. The participants on occasion "play to the camera." However, in most instances they quickly lose interest in the camera when they turn to their assigned task.

Multiple cameras and recording units provide more data, but for the study of most dyadic processes they are not necessary. In fact, they are usually counterproductive. Single camera recordings of dyadic transactions will usually provide a sufficient record. If two cameras and split screen recording facilities are available and if the focus of investigation is triadic interaction, then it may be advisable to record the activity from two different angles. A more adequate record of nonverbal triadic activity can be obtained by locating cameras in two different corners of the room. The frequency and nature of eye contact and other nonverbal activities can more readily be specified from two recordings than from a single recording. However, if multiple visual recordings are made the researcher has more data to manage. If too much data is acquired it can overwhelm the researcher.

If the recording equipment has multiple sound tracks it is advisable to use them. When people interact they often speak simultaneously. It is more difficult to make accurate transcriptions of the auditory activity from single track audio recordings than from multiple track recordings. A single track sound recording is usually adequate for dyadic encounters.

Zoom lens are unnecessary. The objective is to obtain a recording of social encounters, not dramatic closeups of the responses of individuals. Sociological researchers have quite different interests than producers of drama. The objective when recording specimens of social activities is to acquire replicas of social activity that will advance our understanding of social processes and relationships, not to win artistic awards.

PLACEMENT OF EQUIPMENT

If the recorder and monitor are observable to the participants they will be a major distraction. Therefore, the recording units and monitors should be in an adjacent room. Furthermore, one person should remain in the recording room and operate the equipment. It is difficult for one person to both position subjects and operate the equipment. If one person attempts to do both, it increases the likelihood of foul-ups. Furthermore, when one person attempts to fulfill both functions it makes the subjects more conscious of the recording equipment.

If the camera is placed close to the subjects it is more likely to be a distraction than if it is placed several feet away from them. If the camera is 15 to 20 feet away from the participants and "blended in" with other furnishings and if the participants have a challenging task, most will quickly "forget" it.

The microphones can be placed on a table or desk, but if they are hung from the ceiling just above the heads of the participants they are less obtrusive and usually will yield higher quality audio recordings than when placed on a table. A microphone placed on the desk in front of the participants constantly reminds the subjects that they are being recorded. In addition, some subjects may tap on the microphone. That can be irritating when transcribing recordings. It was one subject intermittently tapping on the microphone with a pencil that enticed us to hang the microphones from the ceiling. The tapping was so irritating that it was almost impossible to transcribe the recording.

SINGLE EPISODE SESSIONS

Diagram I displays an arrangement of the laboratory and equipment for a single episode study of dyadic interaction. A room as stark as the one indicated is likely to make participants uncomfortable. The presence of bookshelves, overstuffed chairs and other assorted furnishings will make them feel more at ease. Furthermore, additional furniture can provide a "waiting area" for the first arrivals. A reasonable arrangement is to have the table and chair where the participants will be seated when the session begins in one section of the room, and the rest of the room filled with furniture.

Even when the study is limited to single encounters it is preferable, but not necessary, for the room to have two entries. One for the participants to enter and the other for the positioner to exit from after he has provided the subjects with their instructions. When the room has only a single doorway, it is more likely that log jams will occur.

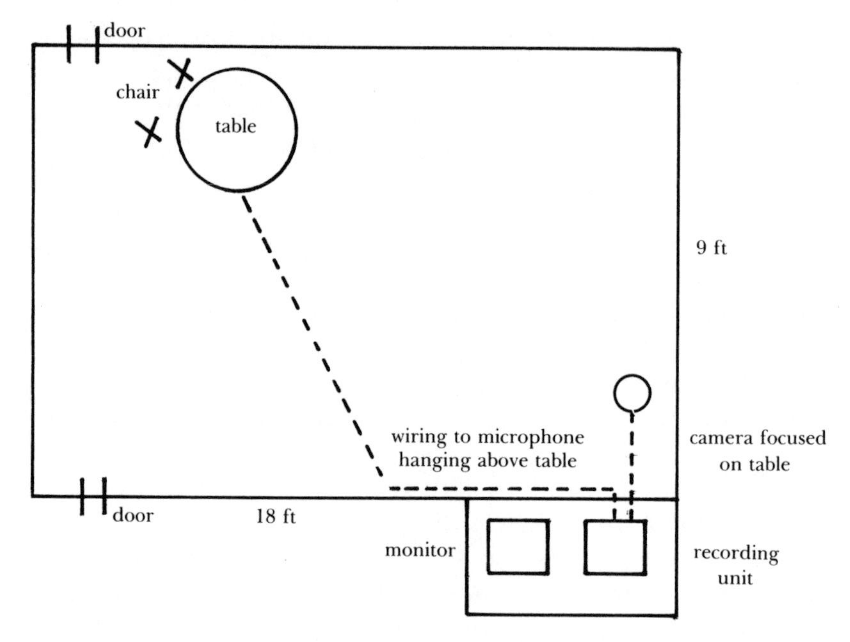

Diagram II. 1. Laboratory Arrangement for Single Episode Dyadic Encounters

It is possible to establish complex contexts in a single room. We completed a study of authority relationships within one room. The only equipment in addition to table and chairs were several sets of tinker toys. The room was arranged in the manner shown in Diagram II.2. When the volunteers appeared to take part they were asked to imagine that the laboratory was a factory and that the purpose of the factory was to produce tinker toy models. Diagrams were provided. They were assigned the identities of boss, workers, and unemployed worker. None of the participants had any difficulty assuming the assigned identities and acting as if they were employed in a factory.

In a similar manner a study of diffusion was completed by asking the participants to imagine the laboratory was a bridge construction site. Again, tinker toys were provided as the construction material. One participant, the cultural carrier, attempted to convince two others to abandon their practice of building post and lintel bridges and to adopt her new procedure for constructing bridges.

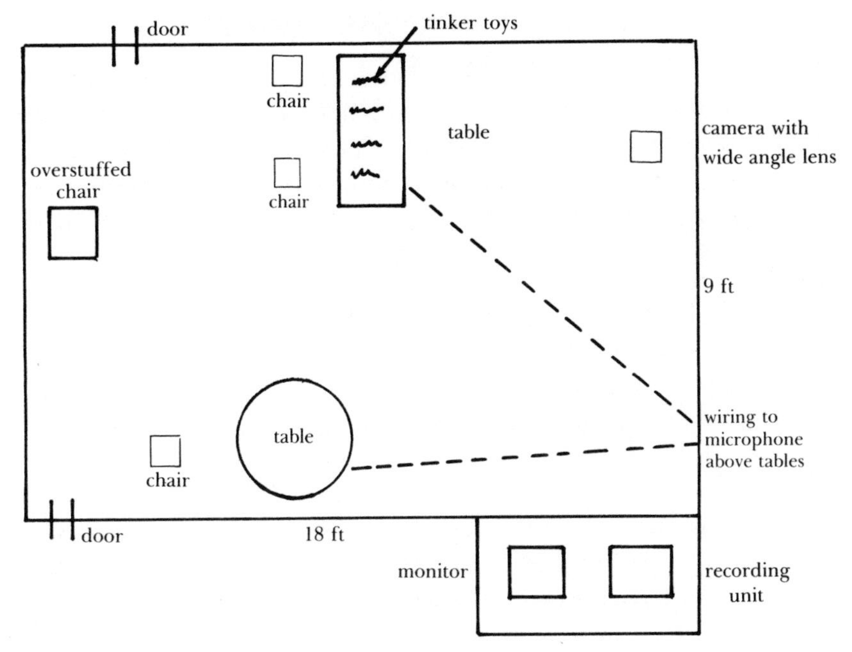

*The arrangement is one used to study authority relationships

Diagram II. 2. Laboratory Arrangement for Episodes for Triadic Encounters*

In these studies a few props and instructions were used to create a context in the laboratory that elicited select specimens of social action. Theatrical directors ask their actors and audiences to imagine the stage and its props are something other than a stage and props. In a similar manner the participants in the laboratory studies of authority and diffusion are asked to imagine the laboratory arrangement and props are something other than a laboratory and tinker toys. The participants in the study of authority relationships were asked to imagine the laboratory was a factory; those of the study of diffusion that the laboratory was a bridge construction site. None had any difficulty in doing so.

With a little imagination a few pieces of equipment, and the cooperation of volunteers, complex social structures can be created within a single room laboratory. The failure to use the sociological imagination often is far more constraining than is limited space and equipment.

MULTIPLE EPISODE SESSIONS

Specimens of many social phenomena can be elicited within a single room; but, to acquire the data necessary to research some social processes it is necessary to use two, three or four rooms. And, of course, sometimes it is necessary to use multiple recording units. However, studies of quite complex social processes can be completed with a single recording unit and two or three rooms.

For example, Wieting (1977) used only one recording unit and three rooms in his study of constancy and change in patterns of problem solving across generations. The sessions were begun by composing triads populated with persons assigned the identities of grandfather, father, and son. At the end of the first episode the grandfather was removed and replaced by a person assigned the identity of son; and, the original father became the grandfather, and the original son become the father. At the beginning of each session the triads were given a problem to solve.

The three participants were seated around a table in the central room. Prior to entering the central room each son was instructed in another room. A third room was required for debriefing the grandfathers after they had "died." Three rooms were required for that study. But, as only the activities that the triad produced while solving the problems were of interest, only one recording unit was necessary.

Some of our more complex studies have been of intergroup negotiations between a representative of the establishment (a dean) and a representative of a partisan group (students). Each of these studies addressed different questions, but essentially the same laboratory arrangement was used for all of them. The arrangement consisted of three interconnecting rooms with a fourth room housing the recording equipment. The central room served as the meeting place for the intergroup negotiations and the dean's office. It was furnished with an impressive desk, file cabinets, telephone and sundry props. One of the secondary rooms served as the office of the vice-president. The volunteers who were to play the part of dean reported to this room. Each of them was told they were to imagine they were a dean at the university and informed about the general context and told of the specific problem that was confronting them. They were also told that the graduate student who was positioning them would play the part of vice president and was the dean's superior.

The three volunteers who were to play the part of protesting students reported to another secondary room. They were greeted by a second graduate student who gave them their instructions and played the part of the dean's secretary. The dean and protesting students were given different but compatible sets of instructions.

After the dean indicated he understood his instructions he was ushered into the central room arranged to replicate a dean's office to await the representative of the protesting students. Then the representative of the protesting students was ushered into the dean's office and introduced to the dean by the positioner of the protesting students. After the intergroup negotiating session each of them returned to their respective home room.

It is necessary for the positioners to control the beginning and ending of episodes. That can be accomplished in a number of ways. In the studies of representation and negotiation the planning sessions of the triads of protesting students were brought to an end when the positioner re-entered the planning room and ushered their representation into the central room. In the first two studies of intergroup negotiations we brought the meetings between the dean and the student representation to an end by having the positioner of the protesting students enter the dean's office and ushering the students' representative back to the planning room. In a later study instead of having the positioner re-enter the central room we used an intercom. After the dean and students' representative had negotiated for eight minutes the positioner of the students, who also served as the dean's secretary, announced over the intercom that the dean had an appointment with the vice-president in a couple of minutes. Then after the two minutes had expired she informed them that the vice-president was waiting for the dean. If the dean and the students' representative did not disengage in two minutes the positioner of the dean who was also playing the part of vice president announced, "Dean ———, I am waiting for you." This arrangement minimized our face-to-face contact with the participants and yet controlled the length of the episodes.

In another study we used an intercom to examine the impact of the constituents' having an independent source of information about the intergroup negotiation meeting on the representative relationship (Katovich, Weiland, and Couch, 1981). At the conclusion of the intergroup meeting the students' representative was delayed in the hallway a few minutes before he was allowed to return to his constituents. In one half of the sessions a member of the research team interviewed the dean about the outcome of the session. The constituents of these groups heard the interview before the representative returned to them.

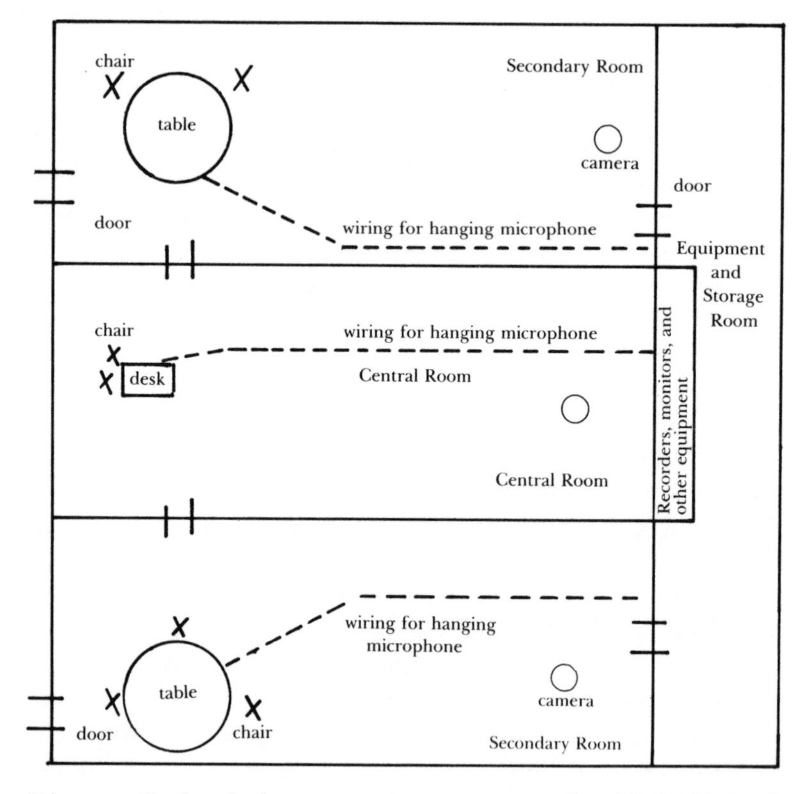

Diagram II. 3. Laboratory Arrangement for Multi Episode Sessions

When the research question requires only single dyadic and triadic encounters it is relatively easy to acquire adequate recordings. On the other hand if it is necessary to record multiple encounters of triads or larger units then the placement of the camera(s) and microphone(s) requires careful consideration. If the sessions are composed of two or more episodes with subjects moving from room to room than the difficulties of obtaining high quality recordings are compounded. Attention must be given to both the problems associated with the movement of participants from room to room and the acquisition of adequate recordings in each room.

GENERAL OBSERVATION

The recording equipment—the camera and microphone—are obtrusive. However, if they are properly placed and blended with other furnishings, and if the volunteers are treated as intelligent persons who are cooperating with the researcher to generate specimens of social action, the obtrusiveness of the recording equipment is far less than most imagine. If researchers use their sociological imaginations when arranging the laboratory it is relatively easy to create contexts within the laboratory that will entice the participants to direct most of their attention to the assigned tasks and be relatively unconcerned about the recording equipment.

The social science laboratory and audio-visual recording devices are powerful tools for the study of social processes and relationships if they are harnessed by the sociological tradition and focused with a sociological imagination. However, if social scientists become too enthralled with the technology they may fail to generate viable data. Some social scientists have been so concerned with being scientific that they have misused the laboratory (Couch, Katovich and Miller, 1987). Some laboratory researchers have not allowed the subjects to interact with each other. Those studies, of course, do not contribute to our understanding of social processes. It is absolutely necessary to establish contexts within the laboratory that allow the participants to interact if data relevant to sociological issues are to be generated. Of course, the nature and length of contact between participants must be contextualized and controlled by researchers if manageable and useful data are to be acquired. The laboratory and equipment, if properly used, will contribute to the generation of specimens of social action which can then be analyzed to advance our understanding of social life.

Recordings for sociological research need to be of sufficient technical quality so they can provide the researcher with information equal to that derived by each of the interactants as they take each other into account in social encounters. Of course there is a difference in the quality of the information acquired by interactants as they take each other into account and the information available to researchers while viewing and listening to recordings into account. However, that difference is counteracted by the fact the researchers can play and replay the recordings whereas those in the situation only experience the actions of the others once.

The power of recordings for social scientists is that they allow researchers to acquire a far more complete record of what transpires than is possible by naked eye and ear observation. Furthermore, the fidelity of recordings is much higher than the either observations through one-way mirrors, field notes, or questionnaire responses. Recordings provide processual data, not static indicators of social processes.

Both the technical and sociological quality of the recordings to be obtained can be checked by those conducting the study running themselves through the programmed sequence and recording their activities. These recordings can be examined to determine if the quality of the recordings is acceptable. Sometimes it will become apparent that the location of the microphone or camera has to be changed in order to obtain adequate recordings. Or, it may become apparent that the furnishings need to be rearranged. One procedure for determining if the quality of the recordings is acceptable is to transcribe a few minutes of the recording of the practice run. If it is difficult to understand the speech or to observe some of the nonverbal gestures then it is necessary to rearrange the laboratory and/or to relocate the recording equipment.

It is as necessary to obtain high-quality audio as it is to obtain high-quality visual recordings. Many users of video technology are enamored with the visual recordings and fail to give sufficient attention to the quality of the audio recordings. Adequate recordings of both visual and auditory phenomena are necessary.

It is much easier to transcribe and analyze high-quality recordings than low-quality recordings. Considerable time and money can be lost when the quality of the recordings is so low that it is difficult to decipher the audio portions of the recordings. However, the completion of significant laboratory studies of social processes does not require the production of studio quality recordings.

Chapter III

Design

If social scientists slavishly imitate the procedures of physicists and biologists when designing laboratory studies they will not acquire data relevant to sociological questions. Social life has qualities that inorganic and organic phenomena do not possess (Couch, 1982). These qualitative differences must be acknowledged and taken into account when designing laboratory studies of social phenomena. One qualitative difference is that human action is temporally structured. Human action not only occurs across time, but in addition, human beings use their pasts to project futures. It is projected futures that structure action in the ongoing present. A second distinctive quality is that whenever human beings establish copresence they attempt to determine each other's intentions. One of the consequences of the temperal dimensions of human conduct is that participants in laboratory studies attempt to assess the intentions of the investigators. Inorganic and organic objects do not exercise intentionality, nor do they attempt to determine the intentions of researchers. These features of social life complicate the tasks of laboratory researchers of social processes. That complication can not be resolved by attempting to eradicate anticipations, intentions, and assessments. If researchers of social processes could eradicate the anticipations and intentions of participants, one of the essential qualities of human action would be ruled out. The data generated would be of no utility to social scientists.

Some social scientists who undertake laboratory studies attempt to eradicate anticipations and intentions when they design laboratory studies. That is impossible. About the only time human beings do not anticipate and exercise intentionality is when they are asleep, unconscious, or alone and let their thoughts drift. Whenever they are acting with others, or with respect to others, anticipations and intentions partially structure the encounters.

Some laboratory researchers create laboratory conditions that make it difficult for their subjects to anticipate the future or to act with intentionality toward the critical stimulus. Psychologists often use the stimuli of mild electric shock and air puffs when they conduct laboratory studies. Each shock and puff of air is somewhat of a surprise. Yet, even in those situations the subjects organize their behavior in part on the basis of their anticipations. These studies provide data for the study of the responses of persons to different sets of stimuli and various sequences of stimuli. However, these studies do not generate data on social processes and social relationships.

Other laboratory researchers attempt to make the anticipations and intentions of the subjects irrelevant to the activity produced in the laboratory. A common procedure is to deceive the volunteers; the participants are told that X is the phenomena under investigation whereas in fact the researcher is attempting to generate data relevant to Y. The volunteers for Milgram's famous studies of obedience were told that the relationship between punishment and learning was the topic under investigation (Milgram, 1963, 1965, 1968).

Both those who design studies to prevent subjects from accurately anticipating future developments and those who presume it is necessary to deceive subjects, do it so that their subjects cannot accurately assess the intentions of the researcher. These researchers assume that in order to conduct scientific laboratory studies of human *action* the participants must be situated in a manner that only allows them to respond. Such procedures do not make the research scientific. In fact those procedures make it unlikely that any data will be generated that will contribute to a greater understanding of social processes and relationships.

Human beings, like all objects, respond to impingements. However, social action is not merely a response or a set of responses. The production of social action requires the exercise of initiation as well as the production of responses. When persons cannot initiate or cannot anticipate each other's actions, they cannot produce social action, nor can they establish social relationships. When it is impossible for persons to anticipate each other's action, the most complex action possible is mutual avoidance, action toward each other, or copresent apathy (Hintz and Couch, 1975: 45). When it is impossible to detect the other's intentions we may act with respect to him, but we cannot act with him.

Therefore, to complete laboratory studies of social processes and relationships it is necessary to provide a context that allows participants to anticipate, act with intentionality, and assess each other's intentions. The task for laboratory researchers of social action is to elicit and focus specific anticipations and intentions, not to eradicate them. It is not necessary, nor is it fruitful, to deceive participants to study social processes in the laboratory.

It is possible to elicit some forms of social activity through deception, but deception has its costs. It complicates the relationship between researchers and participants and is of questionable morality. Even when no deception is planned most volunteers suspect they will be deceived. Consequently, a suspicious awareness context usually prevails between the participants and researchers (Glaser and Strauss, 1964). When the participants are suspicious it produces uncontrolled variation within and across conditions. That makes it difficult to create ideal laboratory conditions. There is little that can be done in the immediate future to control that source of variation. But, it is a factor to keep in mind while designing studies.

Some argue that persons will behave differently when they are aware of what they are doing than when they are unaware. However, when human beings coordinate their actions they usually are aware of what they are doing. They have consciousness of the context, their and others' identities in the context, and have at least some vague idea of the objective(s) of the encounter. In day-to-day encounters some individuals have hidden agendas. For example, when a con artist attempts to fleece a mark he hides his intentions from his intended victim. But, even encounters of that sort are structured by one or more social objectives. All coordinated action is structured by at least one mutually acknowledged social objective. If a social objective is not established people can act with respect to each other, but they cannot act with each other. The same condition holds in the laboratory.

When persons do not know what they are doing—the purpose of their interaction—they may act with respect to each other or establish the purpose of their togetherness as their shared focus and attempt to determine their objective. But, they cannot align their actions to achieve objectives. Unless the study is directed toward the examination of how persons organize themselves in an ambiguous situation, the problem in the designing of studies is not to hide the purpose of the study, but to specify contexts, identities, and objectives that produce two sets of social encounters and that will generate specimens of social processes or relationships to be compared and analyzed.

It is not possible to provide volunteers with complete information about the specific purpose of all studies. Often the only objective structuring the effort of the researcher is to acquire more data on a specific type of social phenomena. But, volunteers can and should be given a general description of the situation they will be asked to be part of and told the topic under investigation. If the study is designed to examine negotiations the recruits should be told that. They will then enter the laboratory context ready to produce that form of social action.

Nearly all volunteers intend to cooperate. It is that fact that allows sociological researchers to effectively use the laboratory to study social processes. If volunteers are told what sort of activity they will be asked to produce it relieves the researcher (positioner) of the task of maintaining a false front. When the nature of the study is made known to the volunteers a more secure and stable relationship between researchers and participants can be established than when the deception is practiced. It simplifies the management of self and participants. In addition, in the long run if social scientists are honest with their volunteers it may lessen the distrust that many have toward social scientists.

THE PROBLEM OF AUTHORITARIANISM

The congruent anticipations and intentions brought to the laboratory by volunteers and researchers creates an authority relationship. When an authority relationship prevails between persons, the authority is accountable for organizing both his own action and the action of the subordinates; reciprocally, the subordinates are accountable for being attentive, responsive, and compliant to the authority (Weiland, 1975; Miller, 1986a, 1986b). The activation of an authority relationship is necessary to create contexts within the laboratory that will elicit relatively pure specimens of various forms of social processes (Sehested and Couch, 1986).

The highly authoritarian nature of the relationship between researchers and participants is recognized by nearly all who have completed laboratory studies of human behavior. Some critics of laboratory research of social phenomena claim that all laboratory findings are thereby of questionable merit. On the other hand, some advocates of laboratory research have offered procedures for minimizing the relationship or correcting for it (Orne, 1962). The more reasonable solution is to recognize the authority relationship and *use* it to exclude extraneous factors and to elicit specific specimens of social action.

Efforts to deny the authority relationship will be counter productive. The relationship cannot be effectively denied. All participants know they are in a subordinate position; if the researcher does not assume command of the situation chaos, not order, will follow. About the only way the authority relationship can be removed from laboratory studies of social processes is for a group of persons to collectively design a study and then use themselves as subjects. Even then when the study is run one or two of them will have to take charge during the actual running of the sessions.

Authority relationships take many different forms. Some are very asymmetrical and enduring while others are only slightly asymmetrical and of short duration. It is not necessary to create a highly authoritarian relationship between researcher and subjects. In fact if a highly authoritarian relationship between the researcher and participants is established it is difficult to elicit other relationships in the laboratory. In highly authoritarian relationships subordinates focus their attention on the superordinate and give very little attention to anything else. Unless the topic under investigation is interaction within authority relationships it is necessary to create contexts wherein the participants will give only minimal attention to the researcher and orient themselves primarily to each other.

The relationship between researchers and participants has some similarities with that between teachers and students. If authority is not exercised in the classroom, learning may occur or the class may devolve into chaos. If authority is judiciously used in the classroom it can enhance the learning experience; if it is capriciously used it is likely to inhibit learning. In like manner, if the relationship is judiciously used in the laboratory, ideal specimens of social action and social relationships can be elicited. If it is crudely exercised or if a relationship approaching tyranny is established, it is likely that the interaction of the participants will be so disjointed that the process or relationship under investigation will be obscured and distorted.

The ideal relationship between researcher and participants has more similarity with that between a director of a theater production and actors than it has with the teacher-student relationship (Katovich, 1984). In the teacher-student relationship the teacher contextualizes the situation and provides the content. Further, when completing routine classroom assignments the relationship between the teacher and each student is the predominant one. In contrast, the director-actors relationship has the primary objective of eliciting a specific set of relationships among the actors. As the relationships between the actors comes to the fore ground the relationship between the director and the actors recedes to the background.

The director of a play is concerned primarily with eliciting specific nuances of relatedness among the actors. The objective of the social scientist is somewhat different. His objective is to establish conditions that will entice participants to produce specific specimens of social action. To accomplish his objective it is necessary to design situations wherein the participants will relate primarily to each other and only secondarily to the researcher.

Volunteers and researchers have already established a tentative relationship before they meet at the laboratory. It is one that has been mutually constructed by the researcher or his delegate and the volunteers. When people volunteer to take part in a laboratory study they commit themselves to adopt a subordinate position. Researchers implicitly commit themselves to act as superordinates. The researcher and each participant have a shared past that frames their encounter when they meet at the laboratory. In contrast, the participants, especially if the sessions are populated by strangers, have only a minimal relationship with each other. About the only relationship they have with each other is their shared indirect relationship with the researcher.

The strength of the relationship between the researcher and each participant and the almost total absence of any relationship between the participants at the beginning of each session makes it necessary for researchers to carefully program their own behavior toward the participants. The relationship between the positioner(s) and the participants is paramount during the opening moments of each session. If that relationship remains the most salient one, only a limited level of relatedness will be established among the participants. The objective of the researcher is to set the stage or establish a context wherein the participants will become attentive and responsive primarily to each other. This can be accomplished by the positioner using his authority to establish the desired context, assign identities, specify objectives, and then to withdraw from the scene. If the positioner remains in the presence of participants, most of them will orient primarily toward him and only secondarily toward other participants.

The primary objective is to formulate a design that will create a context wherein the researchers (positioners) and the volunteers will create a mini-social world of short duration. If the proper context is created, an environment is offered to the volunteers that they will use to produce specimens of social action. The researcher can subsequently analyze the specimens which in turn will yield greater knowledge of some select social phenomena. Those objectives are more likely to be achieved if researchers use the authority relationship with sensitivity to create contexts, but then become part of the background. If researchers are continually interactive with participants it is usually difficult to establish contexts wherein the participants will creatively relate to each other and to the environment offered by the researcher.

THE ESTABLISHMENT OF CONTEXTS

The transactions between positioners and participants and among participants is contextualized by the laboratory and by the awareness that a study of social phenomena is the objective of the convening. The context of "a study" is always the overarching one for both positioners and participants. To elicit the desired specimens of social action it is necessary to produce a context within a context. The content of the context within a context depends on the purpose of the study. If the objective is to study bargaining then the context of a "market" or "exchange situation" is created within the laboratory; if the objective is to study parenting then a parental context is created within the laboratory.

Contexts can be established in a variety of ways. Sometimes a context can be created with a few verbal instructions; other times it is necessary to construct an elaborate lay out, program complex sequences of episodes and to provide participants with extensive instructions. Whatever the content or complexity of the study the objective is to create a context that the participants will accept at least for a short period of time as authentic and use to organize their actions. "The subjects are asked to suspend their disbelief and consider the researcher's environment on his terms" (Katovich, 1984: 51). They are asked to enter an imaginary world offered by the researcher and the laboratory.

In studies of dyadic or triadic interaction limited to single episodes, the context can usually be established with a few simple instructions. For example, in a study that compared the decision making processes of dyads with triads, the participants were seated at a table and asked to pretend they are members of a jury and to render a decision of whether or not a person was guilty of an alleged crime, and if guilty what his sentence should be. The participants were then provided with a transcript of the testimony and left to arrive at a decision.

Studies of more complex phenomena require more complex instructions and a program for the movement of both positioners and participants from episode to episode. When the study requires multi-episode sessions the positioners as well as the participants can be assigned identities within the context. The positioners then became a viable part of the mini-social system created in each session.

A study of authority relationships was conducted by creating a factory within the laboratory and informing the participants that the products they were to produce would be sold to a distributor. The factory consisted of tables arranged as an assembly line and tinker toys. The participants were informed that the head positioner was playing the part of distributor of the finished products. The boss and workers were provided with instructions that included diagrams of the finished product and one half of the bosses were also provided with written instructions.

The participants were informed they had 30 minutes to complete as many models as possible and that each worker would receive a 50¢ bonus for each model completed and the boss would receive a 50¢ bonus for each model that his workers completed that also passed the quality control inspection. They were told that the quality control inspection would be made by the head positioner (distributor). Then approximately 10 minutes after they began the two positioners re-entered the room. The head positioner ran his quality control test of the models completed and paid the boss his 50¢ bonus for any models that passed inspection. Few models passed inspection. In the meantime, the second positioner paid each worker his bonus for each model completed. The two positioners re-entered a second time 20 minutes after the beginning of each session. These procedures provided us with three work periods for each session.

In our studies of intergroup negotiations the participants were scheduled to come to two different rooms. The person who was to play the part of the dean came to one room, the three persons to play the parts of protesting students reported to a different room. A third room was arranged and equipped to serve as the dean's office. The positioner of the dean also played the part of vice president. The dean was informed that after he had met with the students' representative he was to report back to the vice president. Reciprocally, the positioner of the students told them she was also playing the part of the dean's secretary; and, that as soon as they were ready she would show them into the dean's office.

The judicious use of space, a few pieces of furniture, equipment, and the careful programming of contact between positioners and participants can create complex social contexts within the laboratory. It is possible to create a desired context with only verbal instructions, especially if the study is undertaken that requires only one episode. However, control of and variations in spatial locations, furniture, and carefully programmed contacts between participants and positioners can often more effectively establish contexts that are taken seriously by participants than is usually possible when researchers attempt to create contexts with only verbal instructions.

IDENTITY ASSIGNMENT

When the context is limited to a single episode and all participants are assigned the same identity then the context and the relevant identities often can be established simultaneously. In more complex studies it is usually necessary to first establish the context and then assign identities congruent with the context. Even when the study is limited to single episodes if the participants are to be assigned different identities it is sometimes necessary to first establish the context and then to assign each his identity. In those studies that do not require differentiated identities, such as a study designed to compare the decision making process of dyads versus triads, both the context and relevant identities can be established with a few verbal instructions.

In one of our studies of intergroup negotiations the members of the partisan groups were first informed of the general context. They were not assigned specific identities until after they had been given a pseudo-history and were informed about current "social conditions." In that study we wished to examine the impact of early versus late internal differentiation of the groups on the evolution of the representative relationship (Couch and Weiland, 1986). All the partisan groups were composed of three members. The participants were told that they were members of an organization devoted to the promotion of women's athletics, that the university had rebuffed previous efforts to elicit support for women's athletics, and that they had been appointed to a committee by the organization to meet with the university administration to solicit more financial support for women's athletics. In half of the groups, immediately after the establishment of the context and being told they were members of the committee, they were told that the administrator would only meet with one of them. Therefore, it was necessary to select one of them as the person who would meet the administrator. They were asked to write their names on slips of paper and place them in a bowl. The person whose name was drawn was then informed that she would serve as the group's representative. The members of these groups thereby shared the identity of being members of the committee, but were assigned differentiated identities—one would be the representative, the other two would be her constituents.

The other half of the groups were assigned the common identities of members of the committee, but they were not differentiated until after they had completed their planning for the forthcoming meeting with the administrator. Then the same procedure for the assignment of the identities of representative and constituents was used. These procedures established a common context across groups but established two different structural conditions. The evolution and transformation of the representative relationship took two quite different forms (Couch and Weiland, 1986).

Similarly, in a study of authority relationships, first the context of a factory was established. In the low-authority situation the three participants were assigned the identities of boss and two workers. In the high authority situation the four participants were assigned the identities of boss, two workers, and an unemployed worker. Again the assignment of identities was by lot. In the high authority context the boss was informed he had the prerogative of firing one of his workers if he wished and replacing the discharged worker with the unemployed worker.

The assignment of differentiated identities can often be accomplished by lot. However, for some studies it may be advisable to assign identities that are consistent or compatible with their everyday identities. In a study of labor-management negotiations, volunteers were administered a brief questionnaire prior to coming to the laboratory. The participants were assigned identities within the laboratory context consistent with their personal sympathies. Those who indicated that they were not sympathetic with either side composed a pool from which we drew persons who served as mediators.

The major advantages of assigning identities within the laboratory context consistent with identities in the everyday world are: (1) most participants will more firmly situate themselves within the desired context, and (2) most will have a more adequate vocabulary for the enactment of the assigned identities.

Some studies may be most effectively completed by eliciting volunteers who have an established relationship and activating the established identities and relationships within the laboratory. This procedure was followed in a study of parent-child interaction. Parent-child dyads were recruited. When they came to the laboratory we informed them that we were conducting a study of parent-child interaction, instructed the parent on how to perform a task, and then asked the parent to instruct the child. A parental context was created and the participants then related as parent and child in the completion of the assigned objective.

The activation of identities and relationships within the laboratory that are firmly established in everyday life is a viable procedure, but it does have some limitations. One problem with the procedure is that each unit brings with it a distinctive shared past that is not readily observable to those who analyze the recordings. The participants may produce units of social action on the basis of factors that are taken for granted. Therefore, it is often difficult to make a comprehensive analysis of the transactions produced within the laboratory. That limitation can be partially overcome by administering questionnaires or conducting interviews designed to determine the nature of their shared past. However, such procedures will acquire at best only crude measures of their shared past.

OBJECTIVES

All coordinated action is structured by a shared objective or set of objectives. When interactants do not have a social (shared) objective they may act with respect to each other, but they cannot act with each other. To elicit select specimens of coordinated action it is necessary to provide participants with a social objective. The objective may be as simple as achieving consensus on an assigned topic or as complex as negotiating an agreement with an opposing group through a series of intergroup meetings.

The establishment of the context and the assignment of identities establishes parameters, but it is the specification of objectives that focuses the activities of the participants. The objective assigned, of course, must be linked to the context and the identities. For example, in the studies of intergroup negotiations once the context and identities were established the participants were then informed they were to plan for the forthcoming meeting with the opposition and were asked to achieve a settlement that was favorable to their side.

NUMBER OF SESSIONS

It is not necessary to run a large number of sessions in order to acquire sufficient data if the study is well designed. When we first began recording interaction in the laboratory we ran a large number of sessions. The original study of openings was based on 46 dyads—23 stranger dyads and 23 friend dyads (Miller, Hintz, and Couch, 1975). An early study of the cross-sex acquaintance process and decision making generated 44 sessions, each 15 to 20 minutes in duration. To acquire adequate data for most issues it is not necessary to run that many sessions. When large amounts of data are generated researchers are likely to have difficulty in completing an analysis.

The number of sessions, in part, is contingent upon the duration of each session. If each session is limited to a few minutes then it is reasonable to acquire 10 to 12 sessions each in two different contexts; if on the other hand each session is to be 20 or 30 minutes in duration, 5 to 6 sessions in two different contexts will provide about all the data a researcher can manage within a reasonable period of time.

It is far more critical that two different sets of sessions be run than it is to acquire vast quantities of recordings. Unless comparison groups are run it is very difficult to make any definitive statements about the processes or relationship under investigation. Comparison groups can be acquired by either manipulating one dimension of the context, making one variation in the identities assigned, or by giving two sets of groups somewhat different objectives to achieve within the context. In general, it is advisable to vary only one dimension for each study. If more than one dimension is manipulated, it will be almost impossible to assess the significance of any of the dimensions.

NUMBER OF EPISODES

The number of episodes for each session depends upon the issue addressed. Data sufficient for studying many processes can be obtained from single-episode sessions. A study of decision making can be completed by making recordings of two sets of single episode sessions. All that is necessary is to bring together two persons, assign them identities, and confront them with a decision to make and record their interaction.

On the other hand, several episodes are required to complete a study of the transmission of cultural elements across generations. Wieting (1977) initiated sessions of cross-generation transmission of cultural elements by first assigning the identities of grandfather, father, and son to the three participants. Then, at the conclusion of the first episode, the grandfather "died" and was replaced by a fourth person who entered with the identity of son. At the end of the second session the original father, who had become the grandfather, was replaced by a fifth person who entered with the identity of son. The third session still retained one person who was a member of the original triad. It was not until the fourth episode that a historical context was established that was consistent with the identities.

Studies of intergroup negotiations requires at least 3 episodes for each session: the first episode consists of a planning session wherein each group plans for a forthcoming meeting with an opposing group, the second episode, the meeting of the representatives of the two groups; and, the third, of the interaction between the representative and the constituents after the intergroup negotiations have been completed. A study of the evolution and transformation of the representative relationship requires 6 episodes: (1) the first planning by the partisan groups; (2) the meeting of representatives; (3) the postnegotiation accounting of the representatives to their constituents; (4) planning for a second meeting with the opposition; (5) the second meeting of the representatives; and (6) the second postnegotiation accounting of the representatives to their constituents.

LENGTH OF EPISODES

Even when carefully circumscribed social processes are elicited within the laboratory the data are very rich. Episodes of interaction that are 15 to 20 minutes in duration yield so much data that it is often difficult to "get on top" of it. The more extended each episode, the more difficult it is to manage the data. If possible each episode should be limited to a few minutes—preferably not more than 3 to 5 minutes.

The length of each episode is contingent upon the object of investigation. For example, in our studies of intergroup negotiations we allowed each group 8 minutes to plan for their forthcoming meeting with the opposition. Some groups did not complete their planning in the allotted time, but all had at least formulated some plans. In the same studies we allowed only 3 minutes for the accounting episode that followed the intergroup negotiation session. Some of the groups completed their accounting episodes before the 3 minutes expired.

The length of time allowed for episodes can best be determined by pretests. The imposition of a time limitation constrains the participants to be attentive to their assigned objective. If no time limits are imposed some will drift off on other topics. Some, of course, will attend to other issues besides the assigned one even when time limitations are imposed, but less frequently and for shorter periods.

For some studies it is necessary that the participants in each encounter be allowed sufficient time to complete their assigned objective. In other studies the participants can be told that they have only a limited period to complete the assigned task. If the time allotted is such that some will complete the objective while others will not, then those groups that achieve the objective can be compared to those that do not. We specified the elements and structure of interpersonal negotiation by comparing groups that completed an interpersonal negotiation with those that did not (Sink and Couch, 1986).

CONCLUSION

The objective of laboratory studies of social processes is to create a mini-social system within the laboratory that has some degree of authenticity for the participants. Once the phenomena to be investigated has been selected it is then necessary to formulate a design that will entice participants to produce the social action desired in carefully delineated situations. The completion of even simple laboratory studies of social processes is a complex undertaking. Many things can go wrong, and they often do. It is impossible to anticipate everything that will occur when a number of persons convene. The completion of even the simplest studies requires that at least three persons convene—the positioner and two volunteers. In studies of complex relations five to ten persons may have to be convened for each session. Then many things can go wrong.

The successful completion of these studies requires careful programming. In addition, it is necessary to have all the artifacts necessary for the context in place; and, properly functioning recording equipment manned by a competent operator.

The attention of researchers is usually focused primarily on theoretical issues when designing studies. Often only minimal attention is given to the practical problems of setting up the appropriate context. However, the acquisition of viable data requires giving adequate attention to the mundane practical problems of getting participants situated in the desired context. If those who design the study put themselves through the programmed sequences, including making a recording of their activities, it will make them sensitive to the practical problems that are likely to arise. When that is done some unanticipated problems nearly always become apparent. Sometimes it becomes apparent that a given procedure for the assignment of identities is awkward or simply will not create the desired form of relatedness; other times it will become apparent that parts of the instructions are excess baggage. And, if the study requires the participants to manipulate objects, problems associated with that activity are likely to be uncovered.

An examination of the recordings of these dry runs sometimes will uncover flaws in the design of the study as well as reveal practical problems. When that occurs it is necessary to go back to the drawing board and redesign the study or at least modify the design. It often takes longer to properly design a study than it takes to run the study once designed. Generally speaking, time spent on design is time well spent. Hastily designed studies will frequently fail to generate cogent data.

Chapter IV

Populating Sessions

Populating laboratory sessions is usually a fairly routine and simple task. If the selection of participants is guided by a sociological frame of thought and informed with a little sensitivity, volunteers capable of producing the desired specimens of social action can be enticed to participate in laboratory studies with ease. The general objective when recruiting participants is to achieve as much uniformity as possible for each set of sessions, and to minimize variation across sessions, except variation introduced by the researcher. If the population of each session is highly uniform then, ideally at least, the variation in social action across sessions will more clearly reflect the variation specified by the researcher and simplify the analysis of the data.

However, while the objective is to populate each session in as uniform manner as possible, each given session may be populated by diverse individuals. The generation of data for some issues is contingent upon populating each session with diverse individuals. For example, to complete a study of socialization, each session must necessarily be populated by diverse individuals—one who is knowledgeable of the issue at hand and the other who is not. Ideally, the degree of differences between the two—the informed and the uninformed—would be the same for each session. When the degree of difference between the informed and uninformed participants for each session varies from session to session it is more difficult to isolate the consequences of the experimental manipulations.

The general objective when selecting populations is to minimize the extraneous factors that might introduce clutter into the sessions. The clutter can be minimized by recruiting people who are capable of producing the desired forms of behavior, populating the sessions with strangers, controlling the gender, age and other categorical identities of participants, and recruiting potential participants in a manner that makes it likely all will appear as scheduled.

The most obvious criterion employed when selecting participants is: Can they produce the form of social action or social relationship under investigation? To offer an extreme example, young children would not be recruited to participate in a study of intergroup negotiations. Young children are not capable of acting in behalf of others; they do not know how to serve as a representative. If those recruited do not have the ability to understand the context or to enact the assigned identities, the desired specimens of social action will not be elicited.

Sometimes it is desirable to recruit participants with the intention of assigning them identities in the laboratory that is consistent with their respective backgrounds. For example, one study of intergroup negotiations was based on the allocation of student fee monies (Katovich, Weiland, and Couch, 1981). The context we created was one wherein the fraternities received preferential allocations of student fees from the dean of student affairs. We recruited members of fraternities to play the part of dean and nonmembers to be members of the partisan groups. We presumed that fraternity members could more easily assume an identity that called for a defense of fraternities and would have a better vocabulary of motives for defending preferential treatment of fraternities than nonmembers; and, nonmembers could more easily assume an antagonistic standpoint toward fratenities and would be better prepared to argue against the preferential treatment of fraternity members. When the participants have knowledge of the issue and vocabularies for the identities they will be assigned they will more quickly and easily understand the context and activate their assigned identities.

Sometimes one set of sessions might be populated by volunteers who are relatively naive about a given form of social action while another set of sessions might be populated by volunteers who are sophisticated in that form of social action. For example, one might design a study of intergroup negotiations and populate one set of sessions with persons who are experienced intergroup negotiators and populate the other set of sessions with inexperienced people. Then, by comparing the interaction patterns produced by the sophisticated participants with those of units populated with naive participants, the isolation of features that are taken for granted in intergroup negotiations might be more easily accomplished.

In a similar manner, if the objective is to isolate some of the consequences of the structural condition of a unilateral monopoly, one could create the context of a unilateral monopoly within the laboratory, then populate one half of the sessions with naive bargainers and the other half with professional traders. The analysis of the data from the two sets of sessions would probably yield insight into the consequences of unilateral monopoly for experienced bargainers versus its consequences for naive bargainers.

Financial considerations and other factors often constrain the population choices of researchers. Not all questions of interest can be addressed by using college students as subjects although many can. Unless there is reason to believe that college students cannot create the form of social action under examination, one may as well populate the sessions with college students. However, to generate the data required for some questions it is necessary to recruit from other populations. To generate data on some esoteric questions it may be desireable to recruit one's fellow social scientists to serve as subjects.

Sociological laboratory studies are conducted to study generic social processes and relationships. They are not undertaken to estimate the prevalence of social processes and social relationships in a population. Therefore, theoretic sampling (Glaser and Strauss, 1967), not random sampling, informs the selection of participants.

STRANGERS

The continuum from close friends to strangers is one of the most fundamental dimensions of human relatedness. Close friends are embedded with each other, have great knowledge about each other, and can more accurately anticipate each other's intentions. However, friendship is not a unitary relationship; each friendship is distinctive. All friend relationships contain a shared past, but the shared past of each friendship is unique. Some contain elements of antagonism, others are almost solely affiliative, and, still others are complex combinations of affection and antagonisms. Stranger relationships are more unitary than friend relationships.

Each encounter of strangers is unique, but the distinctiveness of each encounter between strangers flows from the context, the categorical identities displayed and noted and the similarities and differences in their common pasts. When strangers create a social encounter, the context, their categorical identities, and presumed common pasts structure their actions. In contrast, when friends create a social encounter they use, in addition to the above factors, their shared past to structure their action.

The variations in the shared pasts of friendships introduces a major source of variation in all encounters between friends, including encounters within a laboratory. If laboratory sessions are populated by strangers there will be less variation across sessions. For this reason, unless the study is designed to examine a form of social action or a social relationship that can only be produced by people with a shared past, it is usually preferable to populate sessions with strangers. Sessions populated with strangers will, generally speaking, be more uniform than sessions populated with friends and acquaintances.

A second reason for populating sessions with strangers is that friends often coordinate their actions by using their shared pasts to anticipate each other's intentions. In contrast, strangers more often publicly inform one another of their intentions. As a consequence the basic elements of sociation that constitute a given form of relatedness usually are more readily observable when sessions are populated by strangers than when they are populated by friends.

A third reason for populating sessions with strangers is that it simplifies the context. Sessions populated by friends are, again generally speaking, far more complex than those populated by strangers. The shared pasts of friends intertwine with the laboratory context and make it more difficult to elicit uncluttered specimens of social action than when the sessions are populated by strangers. The social action produced by stranger dyads and triads in the laboratory is starker, less rich, than that produced by friend dyads and triads. That condition usually makes it easier to isolate the basic elements of forms of social action and relationships.

The production of some forms of social action and relationships is contingent upon the presence of a shared past. For example, if one wishes to study the impact of bargaining within the context of unilateral monopoly on solidary relationships with the impact of bargaining within a context of bilateral monopoly on solidary relationships, it is necessary to populate the sessions with people who have a solidary relationship. The completion of such a study requires either populating the sessions with friends or the generation of solidarity within the laboratory. A reasonable procedure for completing such a study would be to populate each session with dyads of close friends. Strangers do not have a solidary relationship. Only people with a shared past can have a solidary relationship (Sehested, 1975). And, not all people with a shared past have a solidary relationship.

The study of significance of a shared past upon some social processes and relationships can be examined in other ways than by populating the sessions with friends and acquaintances. Studies can be designed so that some groups construct a shared past in the laboratory. When that procedure is followed the members of all sessions are strangers at the beginning of each session. Powell (1986) studied how a shared past impacted upon the diffusion process. He created contexts wherein some groups constructed a shared past within the laboratory while other groups were not provided with the opportunity to construct a shared past. Three different conditions were created. In one, the condition of a three-way shared past was created, all three members practiced constructing bridges out of tinker toys together. After the three had practiced together, one of them was called to another room and given instructions on how to build a catenary arch bridge. She was then brought back to the original room and the three of them were informed that their task was to build a tinker toy bridge 11 feet long.

In the second condition, two members of each triad practiced building bridges together while the third party was taken to another room to wait. She was also given instructions on the alternative procedure for building a bridge. The three were then convened and asked to build a bridge. In that condition, two persons had a shared past while both were strangers to the third person.

In the third condition, two persons practiced as individuals in separate rooms while the third person was instructed in a third room. Then the three convened in the main room and were given their instructions. They all were strangers to each other when they received their bridge building assignment.

The shared pasts generated within a laboratory, such as those based on 10 minutes of practicing bridge building with tinker toys, are of minimal robustness when compared to the shared pasts of life-long friends. However, laboratory generated shared pasts are available for detailed inspection whereas it is impossible for a laboratory researcher to make a detailed inspection of shared pasts constructed outside the laboratory and imported into the laboratory.

The shared pasts of those triads of Powell's study that practiced building bridges together had parallels with the shared pasts of a work team. The brief removal of one of the members for special instruction was in turn parallel to the condition of one of the members of the work team attending a short course on a more effective construction technique and returning to the work team. In both situations, a traditional way of doing things has been established and a novel procedure is introduced by the returning member.

In general, unless a robust shared past is an essential facet of the topic under investigation, the data derived from sessions populated by strangers or by strangers who have constructed a shared past within the laboratory will be more pristine and easier to analyze than that derived from sessions populated by friends. The interaction produced by persons with a robust shared past contains elements that are largely unknowable to the researcher.

The study that isolated the elements and structure of cooperative behavior was completed by populating half of the sessions with dyads of strangers and the other half with dyads of friends. An unanticipated finding was the discovery that friends can construct openings hierarchically. All of the stranger dyads and most of the friend dyads who moved from acting independently to acting interdependently constructed their openings sequentially. They first established reciprocal attention and a shared focus, became socially responsive, and then projected congruent functional identities and a social objective. However, three of the friend dyads constructed their openings hierarchically. They immediately began acting interdependently as soon as they established a shared focus. Each member of these dyads assumed the other would respond as he did upon hearing a call for help in the next room. They did not have to first establish reciprocal attentiveness, then social responsiveness, and then project congruent futures. They responded in unison without first noting how the other was responding. They used their shared pasts to rapidly respond in a unified manner to a call for help.

We learned that persons can use their shared pasts to immediately act in unison through our comparison of the sequentially constructed openings and those produced hierarchically. The significance of shared pasts for the coordination of behavior would not have been detected if all of the sessions had been populated with dyads composed of strangers.

If one is interested in researching how a solidary relationship impacts upon bargaining, then one set of sessions could be composed of strangers and a second set of sessions composed of friends. Then, by comparing and contrasting the bargaining of the two sets of dyads, one can get some insight into how a solidary relationship constrains and structures bargaining.

If one set of sessions is populated with friends it is desirable to recruit sets of friends who have similar backgrounds and are equally friendly. That is difficult. But, at least one should avoid populating some sessions with dyads who have recently become friends and other sessions with people who have been friends for years.

The interaction of strangers, especially interaction in a laboratory, tends to be tentative and shallow. Intense and explosive interaction seldom flows from encounters populated by strangers, although it does on occasion. When sessions are populated with persons who have a robust shared past special problems sometimes arise. One of these is that the preexisting relationship may be the dominant one, not the relationship between the positioner and the participants or relationship between the participants that the researcher plans to elicit. As a consequence, it is usually more difficult to create a context that elicits uncluttered specimens of social action when the sessions are populated with people who know each other.

In addition, when sessions are populated by people with a shared past and the relationship contains hostile sentiments, the activity they produce in the laboratory may be embarassing to themselves or to the researcher. One of the first laboratory studies attempted by the author was of marital conflict. Married couples were recruited and asked to re-enact a recent marital dispute. The study was abandoned after the second session when the reenacted dispute transformed into a bitter marital conflict in the laboratory.

GENDER AND AGE

Nearly everyone acts differently toward a 60-year-old man than toward a 30-year-old one. Similarly, most act differently to a 60-year-old male than to a 60 year old female. The variation in behavior reflects not only the categorical identities of the other, but the relation between one's own categorical identities and the categorical identities of the other. This condition holds for encounters in the laboratory as well as for other encounters. Therefore, unless the design of the study requires systematic variation in the categorical identities of participants, each session should be populated by persons of the same sex and approximately the same age.

The investigation of some processes and relationships can be facilitated by systematically varying the categorical identities of those who participate in each session. Molseed (1987) investigated the emergence of triadic structures in homogeneous versus heterogeneous triads. She populated one fourth of her sessions with three males, one fourth with three females, one fourth with two males and one female, and the other fourth with two females and one male.

RECRUITMENT

Once the study is designed, the equipment in place, and the population selected, it is necessary to entice people to participate and to schedule their appearances. These simple features of laboratory research can be the source of considerable frustration and loss of time. The following suggestions may be helpful.

The recruitment of volunteers is often more difficult than anticipated. If the study is begun before a sufficient pool of volunteers is acquired, then it is necessary to continue recruitment as the study is underway. That can interfere with the effective running of the sessions. Therefore, a sufficient pool of volunteers should be obtained before starting to run the study. A table can be set up at registration to solicit volunteers, forms can be handed out in classrooms, and advertisements for volunteers can be placed in newspapers. Whatever the procedure, it is advisable to recruit more volunteers than one plans to use before beginning the study. It will be impossible to contact some of them and others will have changed their minds between the time they volunteered and when the study is begun.

Once a pool of volunteers has been obtained there remains the problem of getting them to the laboratory. That seems a very simple problem, but some volunteers usually fail to appear when scheduled. The completion of a study is important to the researcher, but to many volunteers it is of little significance. Most have agreed to be subjects to earn a few extra dollars and some have second thoughts. Some have second thoughts between the time they volunteered to serve and when they are contacted to take part; others have second thoughts after being scheduled. No procedure will assure that all will appear as scheduled, but some procedures will result in a lower percentage of no shows than others. If volunteers are merely contacted by telephone and informed they are to appear at the laboratory at a given time there will be a fairly high percentage of no shows.

The first step toward minimizing the number of no shows is to contact the volunteers directly. Messages left with friends, roommates, and family members have a tendency to get lost or at least are not transmitted. Even if the message is transmitted it has less impact than a call from the investigator.

Once contact is made, the participant-to-be should be asked to revalidate his willingness to take part. Those who are pressured into taking part are more likely not to appear as scheduled than those who quickly revalidate their willingness to serve as a subject. Once that is accomplished then the time and place can be established. Each of these, both time and place, should be addressed separately.

First the time can be agreed to. After the volunteer has agreed to appear at a given time, he can then be asked if he has anything else scheduled for that morning, afternoon or evening that might interfere with him appearing as scheduled. Then the scheduler can move on to specifying the location of the laboratory. If the volunteer is asked if he knows the location of the room followed by the scheduler describing the location of the building and the location of the room in the building fewer will get lost.

If the scheduler restates the time and place and informs the volunteer that others are scheduled for the same time at the close of the conversation it makes it somewhat more likely the volunteer will appear when he is scheduled. If he is also informed that if he does not appear it will cause others some inconvenience most will feel obliged to appear as scheduled.

If these procedures are followed the number of no shows will be relatively small, yet there will be some. When the study entails sessions populated by only two or three persons little more can be done. However, for studies that are based on sessions of six or seven persons it is sometimes worthwhile to overschedule for each session. Sometimes that can be made part of the design.

For example, one of our studies compared intergroup negotiations that were mediated with those that were not (Couch and Murabito, 1986). The sessions called for a minimum of six participants—three laborers and three managers. Persons sympathetic to management were assigned the identities of managers; those sympathetic to unions assigned the identities of laborers; and the neutrals composed a pool from which the mediators were drawn. We scheduled seven persons for each session. On those few occasions when one person did not show, the person scheduled to act as mediator was made a member of a group and a non-mediated session was ran.

SUMMARY

The objective of laboratory research is to generate specimens of social action that are relatively uncontaminated. To accomplish that objective it is necessary to carefully design studies. However, no matter how carefully designed the study, if care is not exercised in populating the sessions many contaminates can enter the situations. A little common sense informed by a sociological imagination can prevent that from occurring. In general, sessions composed of strangers will generate purer forms of social action than those populated by acquaintances and friends. Unless the significance of a shared past is under investigation, it is preferable to populate sessions with strangers. Not only are the specimens of social action produced by strangers less contaminated, but they are easier to analyze. Friends and acquaintances will use elements of their shared past to organize their actions; some of these elements are unknowable to the laboratory researcher.

In a similar manner, unless the study is designed to investigate the significance of categorical identities based on age and sex, sessions populated with persons of the same sex and age will provide data that are less contaminated than those composed of persons of different gender and varied ages.

Nearly all college students and most others have at least a vague awareness of laboratory studies of human behavior. Most volunteers are suspicious. Those facts should be kept in mind when recruiting and scheduling participants. Most would-be-volunteers do not completely trust laboratory researchers; and with good reason. Given the beliefs held by most toward laboratory studies of human action about the best that can be done is to be as up front as possible when recruiting and scheduling volunteers. If bargaining processes are the focus of concern volunteers should be told they are being asked to take part in a study of bargaining. When they show up to take part and are asked to bargain they will be less suspicious and anxious. They are thereby more likely to produce uncluttered specimens of social action than if they have been misled or kept uninformed.

The term "role playing" has become part of the popular language. If the study involves the participants assuming an identity and acting within a specified context that can be explained to them. They can be told the identity they will be asked to assume and the role they will be asked to play. It is counterproductive to maintain a closed awareness context to complete laboratory studies. Pretense and suspicion only serves to introduce clutter into the sessions.

The selection of populations, recruitment, and scheduling are relatively routine procedures. However, if care is not exercised errors are likely to be made. At the minimum, these are frustrating and in some cases may invalidate the research effort. The exercise of a little caution and thought can lessen the level of frustration of both researchers and participants and less time and money will be wasted.

Chapter V

Positioning

Some laboratory researchers have been known to don white frocks when greeting and positioning participants (Milgram, 1968). Such garb may assure researchers that they are scientists, but it contributes nothing toward generating valid data. That mode of dress adds clutter; it decreases the likelihood of eliciting pure specimens of social processes and relationships. Unless the purpose of the study is to examine how authority relationships are activated in situations infused with anxiety, laboratory frocks and related paraphernalia are best left in the closet.

The use of formal titles has much the same impact as laboratory frocks. It altercasts the volunteers into a very subordinate position. It is not necessary to do that. Nearly all volunteers present themselves as subordinates willing to follow the directives of the positioners when they report to the laboratory (Sehested and Couch, 1986). Modes of dress and styles of behavior that emphasize the differences between positioners and participants may validate the superior status of the positioners, but they do not contribute to the acquisition of valid data.

Even when volunteers are informed of the nature of the study and greeted by sensitive positioners nearly all will be a little anxious for at least a few moments. They know they are guinea pigs. Most suspect that the study is of something other than what they have been told. Nearly everyone has heard stories of how laboratory researchers deceive subjects. Most of them will be wondering about how they will be tricked and concerned about embarrassing themselves. A few who have taken part in several laboratory studies will be jaded. But, even they will be a little unsure about what is going to happen to them this time. Most positioners, especially inexperienced ones, also suffer from at least a little anxiety. Consequently, when participants and positioners make contact in the laboratory both are usually a little tense.

High levels of anxiety usually result in high levels of clutter. The level of anxiety can usually be lessened by having the same person recruit volunteers, schedule their appearance at the laboratory, and serve as positioner. People with a shared past are usually more at ease with each other than are strangers, especially when the encounters occur in strange situations; and, the laboratory is a strange situation. When the subjects and the positioner have even the minimal shared past of briefly speaking with other, their encounter at the laboratory is on a more secure footing than if they are total strangers.

The positioner activates an authority relationship by introducing himself and taking command of the situation. Laboratory encounters between positioners and participants are contextualized by an authority relationship. If the positioner fails to assume his responsibilities as the authority the volunteers are likely to have doubts about the legitimacy of the research. However, the activiation of the authority relationship need not be done in a heavy handed manner.

THE AWKWARD PERIOD

The period between the appearance of the first volunteer and the "official" beginning of the session is often an awkward time. It is a strange situation; usually the volunteers have little in common with the positioners. Many, both positioners and subjects, find it difficult to pass the time in free and easy chit chat. Nor is it necessarily advisable for the positioner to engage the first arrival in an extended conversation. If the positioner and the first arrival are freely conversing, those arriving later are likely to assume that the positioner and the earlier arrival are acquainted with each other.

The early arrivals can be requested to take a seat and told the session cannot begin until the other volunteer(s) arrive. If magazines and picture books are available most will be relatively confrontable.

If sufficient space is available and if it is critical that participants remain strangers until the sessions begin the volunteers can be scheduled to report to separate rooms. Then when all have arrived they can be ushered into the central room and introduced to each other. One problem with that procedure is that if they are left waiting alone in a room for an extended period they are likely to become tense and/or disgusted. If there is a considerable period of time between the appearance of the first volunteer and the last arrival tenseness can be alleviated by the positioner coming into the waiting rooms every few minutes and informing each person that everyone has not yet arrived.

An alternative procedure is to have all volunteers wait in the same room. If the room is fairly large the furniture can be arranged to minimize interaction between the early arrivals. This arrangement provides volunteers an opportunity to size up the situation and each other. It also removes problems associated with ushering them from room to room. Of course, the disadvantage is that late arrivals may suspect that the early arrivals know each other. The likelihood of eliciting that response can be minimized by arranging the room so that all are seated some distance from each other and providing them with reading material. Then when the late arrivals appear they are less likely to think a relationship exists between those already present.

Whether the participants wait in separate rooms or together in a central room, if the door or doors to the room are left open most will feel more at ease than if they are closed. If they have been waiting in separate rooms when all have arrived they can be ushered into the room or rooms in which the sessions will be held and then the doors be closed. If they have waited in the room in which the sessions are to be held, then when all are present the doors can be closed. That serves as an announcement that the waiting period is over and the study is about to begin. It brackets the encounter.

It is necessary to have all subjects read and sign consent forms and to pay them or make arrangements for payment. These details can be taken care of before volunteers appear at the laboratory or as each person arrives. However, if the positioner waits until all volunteers have arrived before attending to these administrative details then all the participants can fill out the necessary forms at the same time. That operates to put them on an equal footing before the formal part of the study begins and clearly brackets the beginning of the sessions.

PERSONNEL

On the one hand there must be enough positioners to assure that all goes smoothly, but on the other hand the presence of a large number of people can create confusion. One person can usually position the subjects if the study is of dyadic or triadic processes and if each session is completed with a single episode. For example, in a study of dyadic bargaining only one positioner was used. As soon as both participants had arrived the positioner had them sign the consent forms, made arrangements for payment, then asked them to be seated at a table. They were then informed of the context and assigned identities. As soon as the positioner determined that both understood the situation he left the room. The completion of the laboratory sessions of even simple dyadic sessions will be more smoothly accomplished if two people man the laboratory—a positioner and a machine operator. It is difficult for one person to both operate the equipment and position the participants and maintain an orderly flow of participants into and out of the laboratory.

Sometimes it is necessary to use two positioners when running studies of dyadic interaction. A study of parent-child interaction required two positioners. Each parent came to the laboratory with his child. One positioner took charge. She introduced herself and the other positioner, reinformed the parent of the nature of the study. She then informed the parent that we wished him/her to teach his/her child how to play two games. She then instructed the parent how to play the first game. Meanwhile the second positioner entertained the child with some toys. In a few cases the parent brought a second child with them. The machine operator was pressed into double duty; she entertained the second child while the two positioners completed their tasks.

Studies of intergroup negotiations require at the minimum two positioners. In a study of labor-management negotiations the laborers reported to one room and the managers to another. Each session was populated by six or seven persons—three laborers, three managers, and one mediator for the mediated sessions. A positioner was waiting in each of the rooms. When all had arrived they were convened in the central room and all were introduced to each other. The same room served as the meeting room where the representatives later met to conduct intergroup negotiations. Then each triad was ushered back to their planning room. In the mediated sessions, the mediator remained in the central room. The convening in the central room gave all the participants an opportunity to size up the situation. It also familiarized those who were later selected as representatives with the room where they would meet to negotiate. The completion of that study required two positioners for the nonmediated sessions and three for the mediated sessions.

MUTUAL UNDERSTANDING

The laboratory context severely restricts the complexity of information that can be comprehended by participants. Unless caution is exercised it is very easy to expose them to an information overload. When participants are overloaded with information they are likely not to understand the context or to become confused. If they fail to understand the contexts then, of course, the controls the researchers are attempting to implement are ineffective. If they are confused by instructions then the participants are likely to spend the first moments of their sessions attempting to establish a consensual definition of the situation. Simple, brief, and clear instructions that establish a context, assign identities, and specify objectives are all that is required.

If it is necessary to provide participants with information of any complexity it can be made available in writing. For example, in our studies of intergroup negotiations it was necessary to provide each side with fairly complex information. They were given a summary of that information verbally and the information in written form was left with them. They were told that they were free to use any of the information any way they wished in planning for the forthcoming meeting with the opposition.

The criteria to be employed in assessing the positioning of participants is: Do they understand the context, their identities, and their objectives? That can seldom be accomplished by the positioner mechanically reading instructions. To properly set the stage it is necessary for the positioner to be attentive to the participants while informing them of the context, assigning identities, and specifying objectives. If the positioner is attentive to the subjects he can assess their understanding of the instructions. Pauses from time to time provide subjects with opportunities to ask questions and to assimilate the information. Looks of puzzlement can be noted and if there is any doubt about the participants' understanding of the context, their identities, or objectives the positioner can repeat parts of the instructions or restate items to make certain understanding is achieved. The aim is to situate the participants for each session within a clearly understood context, not to give a mechanical and uniform performance. Uniformity of understanding by the participants is the objective, not uniformity of behavior on the part of the positioners.

On occasion it is necessary to elicit an explicit acknowledgement of understanding from the participants. For example, in one study of intergroup negotiations we wanted to assure that the person playing the part of dean—the representative of the establishment—would give serious consideration to the demands of the partisan group representative. Each participant who was assigned the identity of dean was informed that the partisan group had stirred up considerable bad publicity for the university and that future bad publicity was to be avoided. Each dean was also instructed not to make any concessions unless absolutely necessary. After the completion of these general instructions the dean was ushered into his office. After he was seated at his desk he was asked if he had any questions. If he had any, they were answered. Then the positioner who was also playing the part of vice president looked at him and stated, "Remember, I don't want any more bad publicity from this affair." The positioner paused and waited for an acknowledgement. If an acknowledgement was not immediately forthcoming the positioner asked, "Do you understand? I don't want any more bad publicity." The objective was to firmly situate each of the deans in a position so that each of them would give serious attention to threats of bad publicity made by the representative of the partisan group. In some cases that condition was achieved by the positioner making a single statement; in other cases the positioner repeated himself one or more times.

The general rule is to keep the instructions as simple as possible, yet situate all within a shared context, make certain all understand and accept the assigned identities, and provide all with a clearly understood objective.

AN ACQUAINTANCE PERIOD?

Sometimes greater uniformity of context can be established if a brief acquaintance period is scheduled as a distinctive episode for each session. If the study requires only single episode sessions of dyads or triads usually an acquaintance period is unnecessary. However, if the context is rather complex then if an acquaintance period following the signing of consent forms and making arrangements for payment is made part of each session participants can be more securely situated in the desired context.

In our first studies of intergroup negotiations we did not have an acquaintance period. Some of the groups of these studies spent several minutes sizing up the situation and discussing the study after they had been positioned before turning their attention to the assigned objective. That, of course, was a source of clutter. In later studies of intergroup negotiations we made an acquaintance period a part of each session. After they had signed consent forms, been given payment slips, and told where to go to collect their money the positioner excused herself to file the forms. Each triad was left alone for three minutes. The positioner then re-entered the room and began the session. During the acquaintance period the participants typically reintroduced themselves, discussed how they came to take part in the study, wondered about the purpose of the study, exchanged categorical identities, and in general, sized up the situation. Then, when the positioner re-entered the room and gave them instructions, most of these groups immediately turned to their assigned tasks.

We have found that when persons are asked to formulate a collective position on a controversial issue they precede with greater dispatch toward their assigned task when they have an acquaintance period. On the other hand, if the focus of the study in on bargaining between strangers then of course an acquaintance period is not necessary.

DIFFERENTIAL INSTRUCTIONS

Many studies require that members of each session be given different information. When that is necessary, less than a completely open awareness context is created. This is not always a problem. In the study of labor-management negotiations somewhat different information was given to the management and labor groups (Couch and Murabito, 1986). Each unit was aware that while they were receiving instructions the other group was receiving instructions in another room. Some groups suspected that the information given to the other group was different than the information they received. If they asked if the information was different, they were told that it was but that the information the other group received was compatible with what they had. These situations generate some suspicion, but the suspicion generated is analogous to that which prevails in most labor-management negotiations.

Comparison groups can be created by varying the information given to those who populate given sessions. That can be accomplished by giving each individual a distinctive set of instructions in isolation. That will elicit suspicion, but sometimes that is acceptable. However, often it is desirable to provide participants with different instructions without generating suspicion. That can be accomplished by having two positioners give instructions to different persons or sets of persons within the same room.

When we conducted a study of authority relationships we wished to compare authority relationships that contained a "well informed" authority with those that contained a "poorly informed" authority. We provided half of the bosses with considerably more information about how to build the models than we gave the workers. The other bosses were given only a little more information than the workers. A set of general instructions were given to all participants before their identities were assigned. After the assignment of identities, the workers were seated at the assembly line and the boss was taken to his table. Then one positioner read a set of instructions to the workers while another instructed the boss. Both the boss and the workers of each session were aware that each was receiving somewhat different instructions, but neither could determine with certainty the information the other party received.

RE-ENTERING THE SITUATION

When it is necessary to create multiepisode sessions then the positioners must re-enter the scene from time to time. In many cases that is not particularly disruptive. The participants can be told that they have a given time period to complete a task. Then when the time is up the positioner can simply re-enter the room and move them on to the next episode. This procedure was followed in our studies of intergroup negotiations. Each group was informed they had 8 or 10 minutes to plan for the forthcoming meeting with the opposition. After the allotted time had expired the positioner came back into the room and informed them that it was time for their representative to meet with the opposition.

The negotiation meetings of the representatives can be terminated by a positioner partially entering the room where the intergroup episodes are held and informing them that their time is up and they are to return to the rooms where the other members of their groups are waiting. A warning can be issued first, followed by an announcement that it is now time for them to return to their groups. The difficulty with that procedure is if the negotiations become intense they may not disengage. In one session eight requests were issued before the negotiators finally terminated their encounter.

DEBRIEFING

Researchers are obliged to answer any questions the participants have and to ease their transition out of the laboratory context. Occasionally, there are bruised egos that need to be stroked. If positioners are attentive and sensitive to the comments and questions of the participants this can usually be managed without difficulty.

At the conclusion of a session the positioners can re-enter the room, announce that the study is over, and ask the subjects if they have any questions. Subjects most frequently ask about the purpose of the study or how did they do in comparison to other groups.

The first type of question can be answered by re-informing them that the study is of authority, negotiation, or whatever the topic under investigation is and that the study is designed to study the phenomena under two different contexts. They can be told that they took part within one context and that some groups are taking part in another context.

Many participants are concerned about how well they completed the assigned tasks in comparison to other groups. They can be assured that the purpose of the study is not to evaluate persons, but to generate data on social processes and social relationships; that the analysis will focus on comparing the social action produced in two different contexts. Some will express disbelief. On occasion subjects have said things like, "I know you said you were studying negotiating and I guess we negotiated, but what are you really studying?" About all that can be done is to reassure them that the topic under investigation is negotiations.

Even when caution is exercised, on occasion some participants will be a little upset. Some will be upset with those running the study; others will be upset with their fellow participants. When they are upset with those running the study, it is only reasonable for the positioners to accept responsibility for any failures. For example, in a few of our intergroup negotiation sessions some members of the partisan groups accused us of stacking the cards against them. When that accusation was made we agreed with them and stated it was necessary to set up the sessions as we did to acquire the desired data.

The more difficult situation is when the participants become angry with each other. That rarely happens, and when it does the anger is usually minimal. But, on occasion, some feelings of hostility toward others remains after they have discarded their laboratory identities. In one session of the authority study some hostility was generated between the boss and his workers. In the debriefing one of the workers asked in a sneering tone, "Are most bosses as unreasonable as he was?" The person who had played the part of boss glared at the one asking the question. The positioner restated that it was only a role playing situation and added that some bosses were more reasonable than others in both the real world and the laboratory. He then told a joke based on his personal experience and stated that it was time for them to shed their sociological identities and reenter the real world. In this instance the workers were not completely "cooled out." They still harbored some resentment toward their boss. It did not appear that lasting damage had been done to either the workers or the boss. Although if they subsequently met, there would be a minor deposit of ill feeling that they would have to overcome if they were to become friends.

Taking part in these studies is similar to participating in role playing encounters. It can be mildly stigmatizing and can generate some interpersonal animosity. Researchers should be alert to those possibilities and positioners are obliged to destigmatize participants if necessary and defuse any animosity that may have been generated.

TWO EXAMPLES

The following two examples are offered to illustrate the importance of the relationships between positioners and participants for creating the desired social contexts in the laboratory.[1] The first study was one of the earlier studies undertaken in CRIB (Sehested, 1972). That study was relatively unsuccessful in eliciting the desired specimens of social action. The second study was completed later (Weiland, 1977; Couch and Weiland, 1986; Sink and Couch, 1986) after we had acquired some skill in creating contexts in the laboratory. The failure of the first study and the success of the second one were due, in large part, to the differences in the relationships established between positioners and participants. The two studies illustrate the necessity for laboratory researchers to be attuned to how sensitive most participants are to the presence and behavior of positioners.

The first study was undertaken to generate data on how protest groups form. The laboratory was arranged to simulate a factory. Each session was populated with five people—one supervisor and four workers. Three naive participants and two shills composed the population for each session. The assignment of identities was rigged so that one of the shills became the supervisor. Each group was assigned the task of making models of tinker toys; and they were informed that a distributer (the positioner) would pay $1.00 for each model they constructed. In addition, they were told the supervisor would receive her pay by taking a percentage of the money earned by each worker. One-half of the groups was in a high exploitation context where the shill-supervisor took one-half of each workers pay; the other half were in a low exploitation context where the shill-supervisor took one-fourth of each worker's pay.

The positioner left the room as soon as she had completed the instructions for the first work period. After 10 minutes she returned and asked the supervisor what percentage of each worker's pay she was going to take. The positioner than paid the workers and the supervisor. The payment received by the workers ranged from $.50 to $3.00. The supervisors in the high exploitation context made from $3.00–$7.00 each. The supervisors in the low exploitation context received proportionally less.

After the payment was completed the participants were instructed to take a break and were moved from "on line" to a coffee table for a "rest period." The supervisor left the room with the positioner after the four workers were seated at the coffee table. After 5 minutes the supervisor and positioner reentered the room and the workers were asked by the positioner to resume their positions "on line." The second work period was followed by payment in the some ratio as that established at the end of the first work period. Again following payment the workers were asked to be seated at the coffee table. The positioner told the workers that another researcher was planning a study and would like to have some of the same groups participant. The participants were also told the other researcher would like them to list any complaints they had about the study they had just completed. The supervisor and the positioner left the room. The worker-shill did not initiate any suggestions, she was minimally responsive to the comments and questions of the other workers.

One of the objective of the study was to compare the responses of groups to conditions of high and low exploitation. It was, of course, anticipated that more of the groups in the high exploitation context would form a collective protest. None of the groups in either the high or low exploitation context organized a collective protest, although one high exploitation group did suggest changing how the supervisor was paid.

The members of all of the high exploitation groups were well aware of the exploitive nature of their relationship with their supervisor. Several of the individuals of these groups made such statements as "She's got some nerve!" and "She made way more than any of us and she didn't even do any work!" Nonetheless, with the partial exception of the one group that suggested the way the supervisor was to be paid should be changed, none of these groups gave any consideration to a collective protest. The situation failed to generate the desired specimens of social action.

Each session of the second study was populated by four people—one male who was assigned the identity of university dean and three females who were assigned the identities of members of Iowa Organization For Women. The dean was assigned the task of meeting with a representative of IOW which was described as an organization dedicated to advancing feminists' concerns and that the representative that he was to meet with was acting in behalf of IOW and that IOW wanted more university funds to be allocated to women's athletics. He was also told, not to make any allocations unless absolutely necessary.

The three women were met in another room by another positioner. The women participants were introduced to each other and left alone for a three minute acquaintance period. They were then given compatible instructions. They were provided with some "fact sheets" about university finances and the positioner left the room.

Both the participants playing the part of dean and those playing the part of protesting students were provided with a psuedo-history. The dean was told the women had been quite active in stirring up publicity and had earlier requested an increase in the funds allocated to women's athletics, but that they had been told there just was no available money. The women were told that a representative of their organization had met earlier with the dean and had been given the brush off.

The dean was informed that the male positioner was playing the part of vice-president of the university and that after the dean had his meeting with the representative of the women's group he was to report back to the male positioner. The women were informed that their positioner was playing the part of the Dean's secretary. After the women had been instructed their positioner left the room while they planned for their meeting with the dean. After 10 minutes she re-entered the room and ushered the women's representative into the dean's office. There she introduced the two of them and left the room.

After the dean and women's representative had met for 6 minutes the women's positioner announced over an intercom that the dean had another meeting in a couple of minutes. Two minutes later she announced, again over the intercom, that the vice president was waiting for him. If the dean and the representative had not terminated the meeting within another 2 minutes, the male positioner asserted over the intercom, "Dean ———, I am waiting for you." The dean and respresentative, upon terminating their encounter, returned to their respective rooms. The dean to provide a report of the meeting to the vice president, the representative to report to her constituents.

The female positioner returned to the women's planning room 3 minutes later. She asked them to imagine that 3 weeks had passed and gave them some additional information. In the meantime, the dean was provided with compatible information by the male positioner. The dean was then once again ushered into his office to await the arrival of the women's representative. The same sequence was repeated.

The participants in both studies organized their activities within the parameters provided by their positioners. In the first study, the participants established relations analogous to those between workers and supervisors in factories. In the second study, the women organized themselves to confront an opposing party over the allocation of funds for women's athletics; the men behaved as deans confronted by a group calling for modifications in established policies. None of the participants in either study violated the parameters they had been provided with by their positioners.

But, in the first study the workers failed to establish vibrant social relationships among themselves; in contrast, in the second study many of the groups enthusiastically constructed relationships among themselves as they directed their attention to the objectives they had been assigned. In the first study the workers during the "rest periods" became only minimally involved with each other. They made comments about the study, the positioner, and their supervisor but failed to formulate a collective objective. Also, in most groups there were periods of silence as they waited for the rest period to end. In contrast, the protesters in the second study were very attentive and responsive to each other as they planned for the meeting with the dean and when the representative returned and reported upon the outcome of the meetings. In many of the intergroup encounters the dean and the representative became embroiled in heated arguments.

In sum, the participants in the first study failed to produce specimens of social action the study was designed to elicit; the participants in the second study did produce the specimens the study was designed to elicit. The designs of the two studies were quite different so several different factors probably account for the differences in activities generated within the laboratory. At least some of the differences were probably the consequence of the relationships activated between the positioners and participants by the positioners.

The fact that the second study began with an acquaintance period and the first one did not may account for some of the differences. In the first study, as soon as all the participants had arrived the positioner "officially" began the study. In the second, the positioner left the participants on their own resources for a few minutes. The relationships that people established in 3 minutes in the laboratory obviously do not have great emotional depth. Nonetheless, it did provide the participants with a brief opportunity to become acquainted, to size up the situation, and move toward a consensual definition of the situation. It probably eased some of their tensions.

A second factor that probably accounts for some of the differences is that in the first study the workers were assigned positions "on line" and each had tasks that they were to complete as individuals. They could talk with each other, but in fact there was little conversation among them while they were working on line. In contrast, in the second study the task assigned the partisan groups was a collective one. To accomplish the assigned objectives they had to interact with each other.

During the rest periods of the first study the participants were free to interact with each other and they did. However, the primary focus of attention during the rest periods were the difficulties each of them had as individuals building the models, how they became involved in the study and what the study was about. Several of the participants in the high exploitation context made comments about how much money the supervisor had made. But in all groups, but one, the comments were given only a minimal response by other members of the group, ignored, or deflected. The negative comments about the supervisor were usually deflected by some statement like "its just a study" or "if this was for real I'd be ticked off."

Much of the difference in the behavior elicited in the two studies seems to reflect the difference in the nature of the authority relationships established and maintained between the positioners and the participants. In the first study the relationships between the participants and the positioners was far more salient than they were in the second study. The relationships between the positioner and participants in the second study were significant, but they did not prevent the participants from establishing viable relationships among themselves and establishing an intense antagonistic relationship with the dean. The salience of the authority relationship between the positioner and the participants in the first study could have been lessened if the positioner had not re-entered the work room and if the supervisor, instead of the positioner, paid the workers for their products. Had that procedure been used perhaps some of the groups would have organized a collective protest.

The salience of the relationships among the partisan group members and the relationship between them and the dean in the second study is indicated by the fact that several of those groups ignored instructions given to them by the positioner when they were planning for the second meeting with the dean. The members of some of these groups gave greater credence to information the first representative had acquired from the dean in the first intergroup negotiation session than they gave to information provided by the positioner. For example, in the second study before the protest groups began their second planning session they were informed by their positioner that their parent organization, the IOW, had instructed them to demand not less then $75,000 from the dean. That instruction was pushed aside in several of the groups when the woman who had served as the first representative told the others that the dean had said that it would be impossible to make a major change in the amount of money allocated to women's athletics.

Another indication of the vibrancy of the relationships among the partisan group members and between them and the dean is several of the women expressed disappointment when we brought the sessions to an end. In the words of one, "We've got him on the run, we'll get him next time." All of the deans were relieved when they were dismissed.

The success of the second study in generating the desired data indicates that vibrant social relationships can be elicited within the laboratory despite the authority relationship that prevails between participants and positioners. However, in order to accomplish that, it is necessary to carefully control both the amount and nature of the contact between participants and positioners. In addition, if the participants are assigned interesting collective objectives they are more likely to establish relationships among themselves than if they are merely placed in each other's presence and allowed to interact.

CONCLUSIONS

The generation of specimens of social action and social relationships under controlled conditions requires that positioners assume command of the situation. Encounters between positioners and participants occur within an overarching authoritarian relationship infused with some anxiety (Sehested and Couch, 1986). It is mutually understood by both parties that the positioner will frame subsequent interaction between the positioner and participants and among the participants. The primary tasks of the positioner are to provide a context within a context and to make the experiences of the participants as enjoyable as possible.

The positioner provides a specific context, identities congruent with the context and social objectives for the participants. The duties of the participants then become that of creating a temporary "social world" within the laboratory. The construction of these social worlds is a cooperative endeavor. Both the positioner and the participants organize themselves to generate specimens of interaction that will provide the desired data.

The staging of these contexts requires that positioners and participants establish mutually understood contexts, identities, and objectives. The establishment of shared understanding requires some mutual responsiveness between the positioner and participants. The interaction between the positioner and participants situates the participants; the positioner offers a context and a set of identities and the participants willfully accept their identities within the context. Volunteers are treated as cooperative confederates, not as persons to be deceived and manipulated, and not as wooden role players. As noted by another small groups researcher, "An environment once given and a generalized outcome asked for, the areas of task specification and group-ordering are left to the groups themselves" (McFeat, 1974: 174).

When these conditions are met and two different situations are provided there is a high probability that relevant and manageable data will be generated. The creation of these conditions requires that the positioners take charge, but then to minimally intrude upon the temporary social worlds of the participants. The only intrusions are those that assure the effective movement of the participants from one episode to the next within the established context.

The laboratory is used as a stage to elicit ideal and genuine forms of social action that authentically reflect everyday life (Katovich, 1984). The subjects are allowed to interact in as flowing and natural way as is possible, yet within a specified context. The context, identities and objectives are set forth as clearly and simply as possible. The participants are asked to do what they would do within a given context. They are not asked to act like their representative in Congress or as their Congressman's constituents. Rather, they are asked to assume the identities of representatives and constituents and deal with the situation confronting them. If that type of context is established, vibrant specimens of social processes and relationships can be generated in the laboratory.

NOTE

1. The description of the two examples is taken from Sehested and Couch (1986).

Chapter VI

Preparing the Data

Audio-visual recordings of social encounters contain so much data that it is usually impossible to complete an analysis of them by simply viewing and listening to the recordings. If the recordings are of very short episodes—1 or 2 minutes—and consist of only a few encounters from two different contexts, it is may be possible to complete an analysis by viewing the recordings and making detailed notes. However, usually it is necessary to make master tapes and/or transcriptions from the original recordings before an the analysis can be completed. Transcribing the tapes is time consuming, but allows for a more complete and thorough analysis of the data. Even when the recordings are transcribed, the analyst is still confronted with exceedingly rich data, but the data are more manageable.

As the laboratory sessions are ran researchers will note differences in the patterns of behavior produced in the two sets of sessions. For example, when we completed the laboratory sessions of a study of the representative relationship designed to uncover forms of relatedness associated with early versus late selection of representatives in partisan groups, it was readily apparent that the structures constructed by the groups in the two contexts were profoundly different. Despite the readily apparent differences, it was not until after we had made master tapes and transcribed them that we were able to to specify with any precision the differences between the two sets of partisan groups (Couch and Weiland, 1986).

The systematic and precise analysis of the complex processual data retained by recordings requires that steps be taken that allows the analyst to arrange the data so that sets of interactional episodes can be carefully examined. In order to accomplish that the data must be arranged to allow for the "side by side" comparison of specimens of interaction from two different sets of episodes. It is almost impossible to that without making master tapes and transcriptions.

Designing and running laboratory sessions is nearly always enjoyable. The analysis of the data is usually enjoyable, but the preparation of the data for analysis, especially transcribing the episodes, is usually boring. Many researchers are tempted to go directly from completing the laboratory sessions to the analysis of the data or to farm out the task of preparing the data for analysis. Generally speaking, it is a mistake to attempt to complete an analysis without transcriptions and, if the transcribing is to be completed by someone other than the person who is to complete the analysis, it is necessary to give the transcriber detailed instructions and carefully supervise the transcribing. If the analyst takes an active part in the preparation of the recordings for analysis he will nearly always acquire insights into the phenomena under examination that he would not if others prepare the data. The time spent making transcriptions is usually time well spent in the long run.

If the units of social action under examination are of short duration, sometimes the analysis can be completed by studying the master tapes of units of social action extracted from the original recordings. For example, if one wished to undertake an analysis of social closings (Leichty, 1986) and the sessions contained sets of social closings then a master tape could be made by transferring those segments of the recordings that constitute the closings to a master tape. One would then have a master tape that contained only the transactions between the time when one of the interactants indicated that the meeting was about to end to when one or both left the room.

After the master tape has been made then it can be analyzed by viewing and listening to it or the transactions on the master tapes can be transcribed. If the intent is to complete the analysis without transcribing the transactions, the analysis can be facilitated by making two master tapes. One tape would contain the closings produced in one context, and the other the closings produced in another context. If two play-back units are available, the tape containing one set of closings can be put on one unit, and the other tape on the second unit. Such an arrangement would greatly facilitate side-by-side comparisons. Less time would be wasted than when it is necessary to remove one tape from the playback machine in order to view the data on another tape.

Whenever the original recordings contain multiple-episode sessions that are longer than a minute or two each, then both master tapes and transcriptions are usually necessary. If those steps are not taken the researcher will spend so much time locating the data relevant to his question that an analysis may never be completed.

For example, one of our studies of intergroup negotiations consisted of 28 sessions and each of the sessions contained 7 episodes: (1) an acquaintance period, (2) the first planning episode, (3) the first intergroup negotiation between the two representatives, (4) the first accounting episode, (5) the second planning episode, (6) the second intergroup negotiation between the representatives, and (7) the second accounting episode. Each session lasted from between 45 minutes and an hour. It is impossible to analysis that much data with any precision. Therefore, it was necessary to "break up" the data into manageable units. One research report was based on the data obtained from the second negotiation meeting of the representatives (Weiland, 1977), another of the first accounting episode (Couch and Weiland, 1986), and still another of the second planning episode (Sink and Couch, 1986).

The data used to isolate the elements and structure of interpersonal negotiations was derived from the second planning episode of this study (Sink and Couch, 1986). The segments of the original recordings that composed the second planning session were first transferred from the original recordings to master tapes. Each of these episodes was approximately of 8 minutes duration. Even then, the data base consisted of approximately 250 minutes or about 4 hours of audio-visual recordings. The transcripts for each of the episodes were from 8 to sixteen pages. We were still confronted with an exceedingly rich set of data. It would have been impossible to make the necessary side-by-side comparison with any precision, if the recordings had not been transcribed.

TRANSCRIBING

Transcriptions can be made from either the original recordings or from the master tapes. The technical quality of the original recordings is usually superior to that of the master tapes. Thus, it is sometimes easier to note subtle gestures and vocal tones when transcriptions are based on the original recordings. A second advantage of transcribing from the original recordings is that the transcribers will become familiar with the voices of those who populate each session which makes it easier to identify who said what. One of the major disadvantages of transcribing from the original recordings is that there is always the risk that part or all of a tape will be damaged during its transcription. A second factor in favor of transcribing from a master tape is that less time is spent changing and rewinding tapes.

Many transcribers are not sufficiently attuned to the social dimensions to make transcriptions that are adequate for a sociological analysis of the data. The critical phenomena are the transactions between those who populate the sessions, not the acts of individuals. If the recordings are transcribed by people employed only for that purpose, it is absolutely essential that the analysts verify the transcriptions.

Discourse

If talk is more or less continuous in the episodes, then transcriptions can usually be most effectively made by first transcribing all the discourse and then later interlacing the discourse with notations depicting the nonverbal interaction. If there is only a minimal amount of talk, then it is necessary to begin the transcriptions by making extensive notations of the nonverbal behavior. Whichever procedure is followed, it is essential that the transcriber be very attentive to the sequential order of the acts. The complexity and rapidity of social interaction often makes it difficult for the transcriber to determine precisely who did what when. Nonetheless, it is essential to arrange the activities in the correct sequence.

The following example is a confrontation between the representative of a partisan group and the dean taken from one of our studies of intergroup negotiations. The transcript is to be read from left to right to the completion of the first two lines of activity and then moving to the second two lines of activity.

Dean: I could talk to the other members of the administration
Rep: we, eh, don't want more talk.....

Dean: and uh, ah, see if something couldn't be worked out to
Rep: we want action.

Dean: increase your allocation somewhat, but, ah, not to,
Rep: You'd better do something

Dean: not to a hundred thousand dollars.
Rep:

The transcript depicts that on occasion the dean and representative spoke simultaneously. If the dean had discontinued speaking when the representative interjected her comments, the transcript would show exactly where that occurred.

To make adequate transcripts it is often necessary to play and replay the recording several times. Often it is difficult to determine who is responsible for a verbal act. This is especially the case for acts such as "uh, huh," and "hum."

Even when attention is focused primarily on the discourse it is sometimes impossible to decipher exactly what is said. When this is the case, either the notation "inaudible" or "mumbles" is made. The distinction is not trivial. The activity is noted as "inaudible" when the transcriber cannot understand the content of the statement, but it appears that the other subject(s) understood the content. That judgment can usually be made with a fair degree of certainly by noting the subsequent activity of the other subject(s).

The activity is a "mumbles" when it is judged that the other subject was not able to decipher the content of the oral activity, but is aware that the other made a sound of some sort. On occasions understandable discourse trails off into mumbles; on other occasions one interactant mumbles while the other speaks. "Mumbles" indicates the person acted in some fashion with respect to the other, or to the issue at hand, but did not produce understandable content. An "inaudible statement" indicates that one of the participants produced a verbal act that the other understood, but that the content is not understandable to the transcriber. By replaying the recordings most of the discourse that is understandable to the other subjects is also understandable to transcribers. While the other subjects have the advantage of being in the immediate copresence of the speaker, the transcriber has the advantage of replaying the recording. The two tend to cancel each other.

All grunts, uh huhs and similar acts are noted. One can usually note head nods and similar acts that serve the functional equivalent of an "uh huh," while transcribing the discourse. These and other acknowledging acts indicate how responsive the participants are to each other's activity.

Laughter is vocal, but not discourse. Nonetheless, it is usually more efficient to note laughter while transcribing the discourse. The amount and intensity of laughter of course, is highly dependent upon the social context. However, when it is present and there is any interest in depicting the level of solidarity it is essential that careful notation be made of all laughter, groans and other vocal acts as well as the discourse. Laughter in its many different forms is one way that human beings powerfully inform each other how they relate to the other.

Mutual and simultaneous expressions of pleasure and displeasure are commonly expressed by reciprocating smiles, frowns, looks of disgust, giggling, and other combinations. These activities are also important; they communicate. These acts can be, and often are, produced simultaneously with discourse. Often, more than one level of communication occurs at the same time. When laughter, smiles, and similar activity are pervasive within an encounter, after a transcription has been made of the discourse activity it is usually necessary to make another pass through the recordings focusing solely on these behaviors. When laughter, smiling, and frowning are uncommon they can be noted while making transcripts of the discourse behavior.

Nonvocal Activities

Once a transcription of the discourse has been completed it is necessary to focus on nonvocal activity. The attention of the transcriber is focused on what occurs "between" the participants, not on the individuals. For example, if two persons are discussing a topic and one of them is wiggling her foot under the table no note is made of that fact. On the other hand, if while one is speaking the other slides back in her chair, a notation of that movement is made. Only activity that is detectable by the other interactant(s) is noted. If the wiggling of the foot is noted by the other, then, of course, it would be noted in the transcription.

The precise sequence of the nonverbal activity must also be displayed in the transcripts. In order to place the acts in their proper sequential location it is often necessary to replay the recording of rapidly unfolding sequences several times. Not only must the sequential nature of the nonverbal activity be noted, but it must also be properly sequenced with the discourse.

To return to the previous example, the completed transcript of the segment was as follows:

Dean: I could talk to other members of the administration
(looks at rep)
Rep: we, eh, don't want more talk.. . . .
(looks up, makes eye contact)

Dean: and, uh, ah, see if something could be worked out
(breaks eye contact)
Rep: we want action.
(staring at the dean)

Dean: to increase your allocation somewhat, but, ah, not
(makes eye contact and quickly break it)
Rep: You'd better do something.. . . .
(continues staring at dean)

Dean: to, not to a hundred thousand dollars.
Rep:
(leans forward, lightly pounds table with fist)

The above example displays two persons intensely confronting each other. The notations of the nonverbal behavior displays the mood of the encounter more richly and accurately than does the discourse. These interactants are not merely discussing a topic; they are also generating a mood and joustling for position.

The interaction produced by dyads with a limited shared past is impoverished when compared to the activity produced within a triad with an extended shared past. The following transcript is but the first few seconds of the opening produced by a representative and the two constituents immediately after the representative returned from her second meeting with the opposition. The women had completed six encounters—an acquaintance period, planning for first meeting with the opposition, an intergroup meeting, an accounting episode, a second planning, and a second meeting with the opposition. A and C are the two constituents and are engaged in an animated discussion when B, the representative, enters the room for the second accounting episode.

A: (drops pencil turns to B)
B: He wants to raise
(sits down, animated smile, claps hands, rolls eyes to ceiling)
C: (playing with pencil, looks at B)

A: animated laughter
(looks at C, then B, shifts body to orient to B)
B: tuition! animated laughter
(delivered in a shouting voice, makes eye contact with C)
C: animated laughter
(eye contact with B)

A: laughter continues
(still oriented to B)
B: Uhmmm!
(stops laughing, looks down to table, picks up and shuffles papers)
C: laughter continues
(breaks eye contact with B, looks back to B)

A: stops laughing
(smiling and oriented to B)
B: I went in and I said, "Dean, you know they told me.. . . .
(vigorous head shake, hand motion of disgust)
C: continues laughing
(looks at A, looks down)

A: (looks to C as C begins speaking mumbles, orients back to B)
B: yeah
(chopping hand gesture to cut off C, smiles, looks at C, head motion of negation)
C: No, that's a bad outcome.. . . .
(looking at B, shakes head, waves finger)

The example is a rather extreme case. However, it indicates the complexity of the activity that can be produced by persons who have an extended shared past. These three woman had become very involved in the situation and constructed a rather intense solidary relationship in the preceding episodes. Both their level of involvement in the situation and their solidarity is reflected in this transcript. All three began laughing simultaneously as B, the representative shouted "tuition."

In this instance and others like it, transcripts display only some of the dimensions of their activities. To complete an analysis of encounters of this sort it is necessary to examine the recordings several times as well as the transcriptions.

Refining the Transcriptions

After completing the transcriptions of the verbal and nonverbal activity it is necessary to take a somewhat different standpoint toward the recordings and examine them in conjunction with the transcripts. The transcriber is usually very sensitive to concrete acts but is likely to miss some features of the situation due to the rather narrow focus necessary for making accurate transcriptions.

If the recordings are then viewed and listened to with the transcript in hand, certain facets of the interaction will often be detected that escaped notice while making the transcriptions. This step is best completed by viewing and listening to the recording from a distance of several feet. While drafting the transcripts one tends to sit close to the monitor and listen intently. By removing oneself some distance and taking a "gestalt" standpoint toward the activity, events not previously seen as significant often take on significance. For example, when the focus of attention is on small units of activity the transcriber may fail to note that during a given sequence one of the interactants has made gross changes in his body posture displaying disinterest; or that in a triadic encounter two of the participants have become oriented toward each other while giving little or no attention to the third person.

It is not sufficient to make complex and precise notations of the behavior of one person in the presence of others. Rather, the behavior of each is noted in conjunction with the other relevant behavior of all the interactants. It is the establishment, maintenance, transformation, and destruction of relatedness that is of primary concern of social scientists, not the acts or feelings of individuals.

When making transcripts it is necessary to give close attention to the visual attending behavior of each person, noting when A looks at B and when B looks at A, but the critical phenomena are not the visual acts of one person, rather it is unilateral versus reciprocal attending. The establishment and breaking of eye contact and similar *social* activities are the critical phenomena, not gaze orientation per se.

After the transcripts have been completed and the analysis begun it is usually necessary to return to the recordings for two reasons. One, the original transcripts seldom are complete enough for the analysis. Certain types of activity take on added significance as the analysis proceeds and often a more refined notation of the critical activities is required. It is usually necessary for the analyst to reexamine the recordings and "flesh out" the transcripts in terms of his special interests.

Critical transactions sometimes are missed by a conscientious transcriber. One study compared groups that were unanimous on which of the three of them was to serve as the group's representative with groups that were not (Neff, 1975). One triad displayed interactional patterns consistent with other triads that had unanimity on which of them was to serve as representative, but there was nothing in the transcription of that episode indicating that the triad was unanimous on who was to serve as representative. The recording was reexamined. Upon the first reexamination, it did not appear that the transcriber had missed any significant events. Yet at the same time at the end of the episode the three persons displayed patterns of interaction that were similar to other triads that had established unanimity. The recording was examined again. Then it was noted that when the positioner said, "You are now to pick your representative. You may choose your representative in any manner you wish.", a rapidly unfolding sequence of nonverbal acts was produced by the triad. A immediately nodded his head sidewise toward B, C raised his finger from the table and pointed to B, and B nodded forward indicating acceptance of the position. In this instance A and C immediately acted in unison followed very quickly by B's nod of acceptance. Complete agreement on which of them was to be the representative was established in a couple of seconds. None of them spoke, yet it was apparent all three immediately agreed which of them was to be the representative.

In another instance a representative and his constituents were discussing the outcome of preceding intergroup negotiations. The events displayed in the transcript seemed very routine. Then "out of the blue" the representative aggressively asserted, "If you guys don't believe me write Dean ——— and ask him." On the transcript it was noted that a long pause followed this statement. None of the preceding discourse or other events reported on the transcription preceding the outburst appeared to set the platform or call for this action by the representative.

The recording was re-examined. The representative, by his style of delivery and tone of voice in the opening moments of the accounting episode, had adopted a "one-up position" toward his constituents. In the minute or so preceding the representative's assertion the two constituents, by their body posturing (both had slid down in their seats) and facial expressions (both had become stoic), informed the representative that they regarded his veracity as questionable. The two constituents had become actively nonresponsive to their representative's claims. Furthermore, the statement "if you don't believe. . . ." was delivered with sarcasm that had not been detected by the transcriber. In this instance, a conflict between the representative and his two constituents in the universe of touch (tone of voice) and appearance (posturing) had emerged that was not reflected in the transcript.

BIAS OF THE WRITTEN WORD

Occasionally, the conclusions reached when analyzing transcripts are different from those reached when analyzing recordings. When analyzing recordings the analyst is confronted by a continually moving gestalt and exposed to subtle variations in tone of voice and body positioning. Often it is difficult, in fact sometimes impossible, to capture these phenomena in the transcripts. The transcripts display a set of objects—the written word. Each phrase stands out as a distinct entity. In contrast, the recordings display a blend of complex ever changing phenomena.

We became acutely aware of the difference in conclusions that can be reached when the analysis is based primarily on the examination of the transcripts as opposed to one based primarily on listening to and observing the recordings in one of our studies of the representative relationship (Weiland and Couch, 1986). In one context, the constituents had been in the same room observing the meeting between their representative and a representative of the opposition; in the other, the constituents' only source of information about what occurred in the meetings was that provided by the report of their representative. In the first context (the open-awareness context), the transcriptions contained elaborate notations of body movement, many instances of two or three persons speaking simultaneously, and often the participants did not complete their speech acts. In contrast, in the latter situation (closed-awareness contexts) there were few notations of body movement, few instances of interruptions, and few instances of incomplete speech acts. The transcriptions of the open-awareness groups suggested chaos and disorder; the transcriptions of the closed-awareness triads indicated some tensions and hostility, but generally speaking a rational and orderly series of events.

The researcher, working primarily from the transcriptions, concluded that the interaction in the open-awareness contacts was more strained and disjointed than the interaction in the closed-awareness contexts. The observations based on the written transcriptions suggested that the relationship between constituents and their representatives in the open-awareness groups were more tenuous than those between the representative and constituents in the closed-awareness groups. In contrast the researcher who made an analysis primarily on the basis of observing the recordings concluded almost the opposite.

Both researchers subsequently reanalyzed both the transcripts and recordings. The incompatible conclusions were easily resolved. In the open-awareness contexts the constituents vigorously attempted to display their support for their representative. They often made disjunctive gestures, they stepped on each other's lines, but the tone of voice and "openness" of their demeanor toward the representative informed all that they were supportive of their representative. In contrast, in the closed-awareness context many of the constituents were actively nonresponsive toward their representative—they displayed alienation. When either the representative or one of the constituents spoke in the closed-awareness triads the statements were typically completed, but often the constituents' only responses were blank stares. Consequently, the transcripts of these recordings appeared more orderly and routine whereas the transcripts of the recordings of the open-awareness groups appeared disorderly and conflict ridden. The open-awareness groups did have more instances of conflict but the conflict was always contextualized by activities in the universe of touch (Leichty, 1975) and appearance (Stone, 1962) that informed all that they were in this together. In contrast, the tone of voice and lack of responsiveness in the closed awareness groups indicated alienation of the constituents from their representative.

The conclusion to be drawn is that often both an analysis of the transcripts and recordings is necessary to make a valid characterization of the patterns of relatedness that are established within groups. If attention is given only to the transcripts or only to the recordings an incomplete and to a certain extent an inaccurate analysis is possible.

OVER-CONCRETIZING

Some social scientists become scientistic when they prepare data for analysis. Recordings make it possible to electronically measure tonal oscillations. It is also possible to use a grid system in conjunction with the television monitor that will allow for the specification of the amount and direction of the body movement of each interactant. It is possible to note that a person moved his arm 4½ inches and rotated it 20 degrees. Transcriptions of this sort are of no utility for a sociological analysis. Such procedures do not measure social action; they do not contribute to the formulation of principles of social phenomena.

The precision of measurement required for analysis is the same as that required to be an effective interactant. When human beings interact they observe, listen to, and sometimes touch each other. In the process they note each other's behavior, assess each other's standpoints and attempt to ferret out each other's intentions. They do not note whether the other nodded his head 3½ inches or 3¾ inches forward. The critical observations for a sociological analysis are those that indicate the nature of the relatedness established by the interactants and the relationships the groups establish with their environment, not the amount or direction of physical movement. The completion of a sociological analysis requires noting the acts people make toward, away from, and with each other. Social bondedness and social action, not physical movement are the foci of attention when making a sociological analysis.

The objective of sociological analysis is to specify the elements and structure of various forms of social activity, various forms of social relationships, and their consequences. Therefore, the transcripts must display the activity in a manner that will facilitate that objective. It may be of interest that the tonal quality of the statement "thank you" can be displayed on a cathode ray tube and the similarities and differences in the blips produced by each "thank you" can be noted. However, the more important question is: Was the "thank you" delivered with biting sarcasm that was mutually recognized or was it a sincere "thank you?" That can only be specified by noting how the act fits in with preceding and simultaneous acts.

CONCLUSIONS

Transcribing recordings of specimens of social action is a time consuming activity, but it often is very informative. To render recordings into transcripts requires the transcriber to be very attentive to the social events displayed. It is very easy for a researcher to slip into a passive viewer standpoint when studying recordings. To transcribe recordings it is necessary to be actively attentive. As a consequence, the transcriber is likely to note acts when making transcriptions that may go unobserved when the analysis is based on only the recordings.

Many comparisons can be made much quicker when transcriptions are available than they can be when only recordings are available. A researcher can leaf through sets of transcriptions much more rapidly than he can examine the recordings of two sets of episodes. The time saved is often more than equivalent to the time required to make the transcriptions. Furthermore, in most cases it is easier to make precise and detailed comparison on the basis on transcripts than it is when the analysis is limited to studying the recordings.

Chapter VII

A Sociological Standpoint

The sociological analyses of recorded specimens of social action requires analysts to simultaneously attend to the actions of two or more people across time. If the study is properly designed the laboratory controls minimize the clutter and simplify the phenomena that must be given attention, but even so, analysts of audio-visual recordings confront exceedingly rich data. Transcriptions allow for the slow and reflective examination of the transactions and thereby lessen the burden. But, unless analysts approach the data well armed with viable sociological concepts that direct attention to social events, they are likely to resort to counting the acts of individuals or noting the reciprocating acts of individuals instead of analyzing social transactions.

We all have a wealth of experience in social interaction. One might conclude that we all thereby have a sound practical background for a sociological analysis of social interaction. However, such is not the case. Most of us usually adopt a standpoint that is essentially psychological when we analyze our everyday social experiences. As we interact with another person our primary focus of attention is the other person not our actions in conjunction with the actions of that person. We attend to others to assess their intentions, sentiments, and interests. We then use the gleaned information to organize our behavior toward or with the other person.

We also attend to our own activities. However, our monitoring of ourselves is so habitual that we are relatively unconscious of it. Sometimes we retrospectively analyze our own behavior, but usually when we are reflective about our own behavior the focus of attention is again that of an individual—ourself.

On occasions we attend to dyads and larger units in our everyday lives. We note how well or poorly two children play with each other, how smoothly an athletic team executes plays, and how well two workers perform as a unit. When we note the transactions between members of a group in our everyday life we usually limit our analysis to making an assessment of how well the members of a unit work together. Whenever we make observations of that sort we implicitly adopt a sociological standpoint. However, we usually do not attempt to formulate principles of social life when we make assessments of everyday social encounters.

Many find it difficult to maintain a sociological standpoint when they give sustained attention to human action. Instead of continuously making the dyad our field of observation we often focus our attention on the actions of one person at a time. When one member of the dyad speaks we tend to focus our attention on him and for the moment ignore the actions of the other. Speaking, of course, tends to be sequenced. However, the task of the sociological analyst is to note the how the simultaneous actions of individuals fit together to produce social acts. That requires attending to the speaker and listener simultaneously.

The use of transcripts and the fact that video recordings can be replayed facilitate the analysis of social activity. However, the replay feature of video recordings and transcripts are a double-edged sword. They sometimes entice researchers to narrow their attention so that they attend only to the acts of one individual at a time. Then the analyst is likely to make detailed notations of the acts of each individual. When only the acts of individuals, not social acts, are the focus of attention it is impossible to complete a sociological analysis.

The visual field offered by a 24 by 24 inch television screen is much smaller than the visual field offered by two persons in live face-to-face interaction. The smallness of the visual scope of television also facilitates making social transactions the observational unit. Yet, even when the observations are of video displays of interaction most viewers tend to focus their attention on the speaker. However, if analysts make a self-conscious effort to make the actions of the dyad or triad the focus of attention, with practice it will become second nature.

The objective when making a sociological analysis is not to note the number of times each person acknowledges the activity of another, but to note and characterize the nature of the relatedness established between persons as they act toward and with each other and respond to each other. Specifically, the objective is not to note the number of "uh huhs" offered by each interactant but to note the nature and intensity of the bondedness established by the members of a dyad as they act toward, respond to each other, and act in unison toward their environment.

Often, it is necessary to replay a segment of a recording to determine if an individual committed an act or to decipher the significance of an act. However, that is only done to determine how a given act fits with other acts. The specification of the presence of a given act is not the end of the analysis, but only one step in the process of specifying the relatedness between interactants.

Many sociologists have generated laboratory data, but few of them have developed analytic procedures that make social acts the unit of analysis. Instead, most laboratory researchers have employed analytic procedures that direct attention to the acts of individuals, the products of individual acts, the products of social action, or the reciprocating acts of individuals. The pioneers of laboratory research on social phenomena (Sherif, 1935, 1936; Lewin, Lippet, and White, 1939; Bales, 1950, 1968; Hare, Borgotta, and Bales, 1955) did not have the benefit of audio-visual recording equipment. They had to rely on other procedures to transform the phenomena generated within their laboratories into data. Some made notations of the activities of their subjects (Lewin, Lippet, and White, 1939; Bales, 1950; Swanson, 1953). Others noted the cultural products produced by their subjects (Sherif, 1935, 1936; Rose and Felton, 1955).

Bales (1950) developed one of the most comprehensive procedures for coding the directly observed behavior of laboratory subjects. Some of the acts noted by Bales' Interpersonal Process Analysis system were: gives an opinion, makes a suggestion, disagrees, and gives support. This and similar procedures code the acts of individuals not units of social action. The coding procedures devised by Bales also transforms processual phenomena into static data. Neither social events, reciprocating acts, nor the sequential order of social events were noted by Bales' Interaction Process Analysis. That type of analysis provides some knowledge about the actions of individuals within a group context, but little about social processes or relationships. In short, that notation system fails to take into account the processual and social nature of human encounters.

Other laboratory researchers (Mishler and Waxler, 1968; Lennard and Bernstein, 1966) have made audio recordings of conversations and developed refined procedures for categorizing vocal acts. However, most of these researchers also employed a mode of analysis that transformed processual phenomena into static entities. They failed to retain the social and processual qualities of social action when they analyzed their data.

Several students of social interaction have made audio recordings of naturally occurring conversations and analyzed those recordings (Schegloff, 1968; Schegloff and Sacks, 1973; Jefferson 1972; Zimmerman and West, 1975). Much of that research has been based on the analysis of telephone conversations (Schegloff, 1968; Schegloff and Sacks, 1973; Schegloff, 1977). Audio recordings, of course, only provide auditory data, they do not display nonvocal activity. Vocal interaction usually takes the form of reciprocating acts. In contrast, in face-to-face encounters interactants often simultaneously communicate in discourse, appearance, and touch. The procedures developed to analysis vocal interaction consequently are not adequate for analyzing face-to-face encounters. However, one of the distinctive features of this research has been a concern with the sequential order of reciprocating acts.

The systematic and detailed observation, notation, and analysis of the reciprocating behavior of individuals has merit, but to complete a sociological analysis of face-to-face interaction it is necessary to note the nonvocal activities as well as the vocal activities. The analyst must simultaneously note what two people do with, toward, and for each other through time; how do they fit together their individual lines of action to produce units of social action and social relationships? It is necessary to note how the participants communicate with each other and the elements of sociation they jointly produce as they coordinate their actions and activate social relationships. Such analyses can only be completed by noting both the vocal and nonvocal activity of dyads, triads, and larger units across time.

THE UNIVERSES OF COMMUNICATION

When we cannot communicate with another, we cannot act with him. The reciprocal display and acquisition of information—communication—is the foundation of all social action. Therefore the beginning point of a sociological analyses of social action is noting how the interactants inform each other, establish shared understandings, and establish consensual definitions of situations. Of course, in some encounters interactants misinform each other, sometimes fail to understand each other despite their best efforts to do so, and frequently become embroiled in conflicts as each attempts to foist her definition of the situation on the other. Nonetheless, communicative acts are the foundation of social action. Communicative acts must be attended to if a sociological analysis is to be completed.

The analysis of social processes is compounded by the fact that interactants can simultaneously communicate with each other; each person can receive and transmit information at the same time. Communication is often equated with discourse (speech). But, in face-to-face encounters people typically inform each other of their intentions, sentiments and interests through appearance (Stone, 1962) and touch (Leichty, 1975) as well as through discourse (Mead, 1934). These three universes of communication are usually complexly intertwined as people coordinate their actions in social encounters. That is the case for social encounters produced in the laboratory as well as those constructed outside the laboratory. Whenever we make social contact by appearing in each other's visual field we announce identities in the universe of appearance and implicitly call for others to agree with the self-categorization offered (Stone, 1962). These static dimensions of appearance are usually offered and accepted in the opening moments of an encounter and become part of the taken for granted background of the encounter. Our clothing, hair style, facial make up, and other elements of the universe of appearance informs others of how we locate ourselves within the social fabric.

Other dimensions of the universe of appearance are dynamic. These include movements from one location to another, gaze orientation, and body positioning. These dynamic dimensions of the universe of appearance continuously change within social encounters. People lean toward or withdraw from each other as they interact; they focus their attention on the other or let their gaze wander; or, they sit at attention or slump in their chairs. These activities inform others of shifts in attention and the levels of involvement in the task and attraction toward or repulsion from each other. It is as necessary to make note of these communicative acts as it is to note speech acts to complete an analysis of specimens of social action.

Interactants also inform each other of their attractions, repulsions, agreements or disagreements and levels of involvement through the universe of touch. Lovers routinely touch each other as they converse; strangers seldom do and if they do they usually apologize for intruding upon each other. Tone of voice, laughter, smiles, frowns, rapidity of response, and tactile contact are universe of touch phenomena (Leichty, 1975). These activities also must be noted when analyzing social transactions.

Discourse, the dynamic aspects of appearance, and the universe of touch are complexly intertwined in nearly all face-to-face encounters. Video recordings provide researchers with data sets that display the communicative acts of all three universes of communication. The analysis of all specimens of social action requires the analyst to be sensitive to the communicative acts produced in all three universes. Usually the information displayed in the three universes of communication is congruent. For example, when a person says "three" in response to a query and simultaneously holds up three fingers the same information is displayed in two different modes. However, in some instances the information displayed is incongruent as when a person states he is interested, but then turns his back on the speaker. Sometimes, in order to complete an analysis it is necessary to note the congruency or incongruency of the communicative acts produced in different universes. Then the intertwinnings of the universes of communication can be examined.

For some purposes communication in the different universes can be treated as functionally equivalent. For example, in the analysis that resulted in the specification of the elements and structure of openings some of the acts in the three universes of communication were treated as functionally equivalent (Miller, Hintz, and Couch, 1975). Some of the dyads of that study established reciprocal attention in discourse, others in appearance and a few dyads established reciprocal attention through touch. When reciprocal attention was established through discourse it typically took the following form:

A: "Did you hear that?"
B: "Yeah."

In other dyads reciprocal attention was established visually, in the universe of appearance, by the members of the dyad making eye contact upon hearing the plea for help. In a few cases reciprocal attention was established by one person touching the arm of the other. As might be expected the establishment of reciprocal attention through touch only occurred within dyads composed of friends.

The objective of that study was the specification of the elements of sociation produced when persons moved from acting independently to acting interdependently. Some of the acts in the three universes are functionally equivalent in the creation of elements of sociation, but they are not functionally equivalent in the emotions elicited. To touch another conveys greater intimacy than to call for another's attention by a speech act.

It is impossible to make an adequate analysis of social processes if attention is restricted to discourse. For example, in one transaction between a representative and his constituents the representative claimed success in the intergroup negotiations. One of the constituents retorted, "Right, Jack, right." The statement was delivered in a bitingly sarcastic tone. And, the representative's name was not Jack. Furthermore, as soon as the constituent had made his sarcastic comment, the representative glared at him. In this instance the representative and constituent established a form of relatedness by tone of voice—a universe of touch phenomenon and glaring—a universe of appearance phenomenon—not by the content of the discourse. If the same statement had been made to a person whose name was Jack in an enthusiastic tone the relatedness established between the constituent and the representative would have been entirely different.

In general, once coordinated action is underway, interactants maintain and modify the nature of their relatedness by the dynamic aspects of the universe of appearance and touch. Shifts in location, body positioning, tone of voice, rapidity of response, and touching or not touching communicate the type of relatedness that prevails between interactants. Social relationships are routinely reaffirmed, modified, and destroyed by communication via appearance and touch as well as through discourse.

People can and do inform each other of their relatedness in discourse. So long as a relationship is a smooth one, persons usually do not explicitly discuss it. When there is some disjunctiveness in a relationship, those who compose the relationship may attempt to reaffirm or modify the relationship by discussing it. They establish how they are to relate to one another in the future as their shared focus and negotiate their interpersonal relationship (Sink and Couch, 1986). Interpersonal negotiations are contextualized by people with a relationship mutually acknowledging that they differ on how they should relate to each other and then discussing their differences. Mutually recognized differences may be communicated in the universe of touch, by tone of voice or slowness of response. But, the resolution of the mutually recognized differences and the formulation of an alternative mode of relatedness is usually accomplished in discourse.

The intensity of relationships is often conveyed through the universe of touch and appearance as interactants attend to shared foci and social objectives in discourse. For example, in our studies of the representative relationship the participants prepared for the forthcoming meeting with the opposition by discussing alternative plans of action. In the process of discussing their plans, the members of the groups indicated their agreement or disagreement with each other's proposal by tone of voice, smiles, or frowns, and rapidity and intensity of response to each other's suggestions.

In a study of parent-child relationships it was observed that the parent and child of each dyad attended to the tasks at hand primarily through discourse and manipulation of the objects. The parent typically instructed the child how to accomplish the assigned tasks by speaking to the child and demonstrating how the objects could be fitted together. Simultaneously, the parent and child continuously informed each other and observers of their relationship through the universe of touch. Some parents and children snuggled against each other as they attended to the assigned tasks; others seldom touched each other; and, some laughed in unison as they completed their tasks while others maintained a somber tone.

PRIMITIVE ELEMENTS OF SOCIATION

As interactants communicate they establish, maintain and destroy elements of sociation, how they relate to one another. Each element of sociation is the consequence of joint activity; one person cannot establish an element of sociation. One person may initiate the construction of an element, but at the minimum another person must respond to the initiation before an element of sociation is produced. Diagram VII.1. displays the primitive elements of sociation that must be created before or simultaneously with the production of action toward a social objective. Interactants become implicated with each other in social encounters by establishing elements of sociation. In some occasions they are only minimally implicated with each other as they indifferently attend and respond to each other; other times they are intensely implicated with each other as they focus their attention upon each other and act toward or with each other.

These primitive elements of sociation can be established, maintained and modified through discourse, appearance or touch. But, in all cases elements of sociation are social creations. Reciprocally acknowledged attention can only be created by two or more persons. One person can attend to another, and in a sense when that occurs, a relation between two persons is established. However, if they are to become mutually implicated, the second person must also attend to the first person, and both must acknowledge each other's attention. Unless reciprocally acknowledged attention is established, the most complex *social* action they can take is mutual avoidance; they cannot fit to-

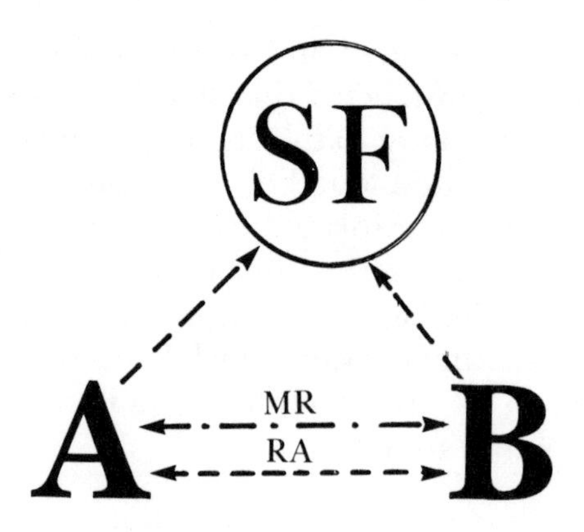

Notes:
RA = Reciprocal Attention
MR = Mutual Responsiveness
SF = Shared Focus
--- = Attentiveness
—.— = Responsiveness

Diagram VII. 1. Elements of Sociation Necessary To Become Mutually Implicated

gether their individual lines of action to produce cooperative action.

To sustain an encounter interactants must be socially responsive. Each must note the other's action in the ongoing present and incorporate the actions of the other into their own action. Social responsiveness takes essentially two distinctive forms—bilateral responsiveness and mutual responsiveness (Couch, 1986b). Bilateral responsiveness is the more primitive form. People are bilaterally responsive when they note each other's action and then organize their action with respect to the other but not with the other. When people accommodate to each other upon meeting and passing by each other in the hallway they are bilaterally responsive. Each notes the other's action and responds to the other to avoid infringing upon him.

People are mutually responsive when they note each other's action and respond to act with the other. When friends make contact in the hallway they usually construct at least a minimal level of mutual responsiveness. They typically exchange greetings and thereby become mutually responsive. Each informs the other that the other's presence and/or action is significant in how one organizes his own behavior.

Interactants can establish both types of relatedness simultaneously. For example, when friends meet and pass by each other in the hallway they can be both bilaterally and mutually responsive. They can adjust to each other's presence and act to allow the other to pass by without impediment, yet at the same time by exchanging greetings they are mutually responsive. The degree of social responsiveness produced can vary from a mild level as when two acquaintances curtly nod to each other to an intense level when two friends greet each other with beaming smiles and enthusiastic hellos.

One of the features of social conduct that is the source of complications for analysts of social processes is that interactants are capable of constructing two or more modes of relatedness at the same time. For example, when members of partisan groups negotiated their differences they sometimes made biting comments about each other's proposals while smiling at each other. In such transactions they informed each other that they disagreed with each other, but at the same time also informed each other that they were not angry, or at least not too angry, at the other. On other occasions, when interactants dispute with each other they laugh in unison. In such transactions they simultaneously conflict and reaffirm their solidary relationship.

The production of all units of cooperative action requires persons to establish a shared focus as well as be attentive and responsive to each other. A shared focus is established when two people attend to some event or object and have shared awareness that both are attending to the same event of object. A shared focus can be anything—a loud noise, the family dog, a sliver in one person's finger, or a philosophical tradition. Accommodative encounters, conflicts and predator-prey encounters in their simplest form require only that persons attend and respond to each other, they do not require the establishment of a shared focus (Couch, 1986b).

Participants in laboratory studies are usually provided with a set of foci by the positioners. Typically once the positioner withdraws they jointly attend to one or more of the foci provided by the positioner. However, once interaction is enjoined then they jointly move from one shared focus to another. Within some encounters people rapidly and smoothly move from one shared focus to another; in others they awkwardly jump from one shared focus to another; and, in still other encounters, interactants remain riveted to a specific shared focus for several minutes.

One moment participants in a laboratory study may attend to written instructions left with them; the next, they may jointly shift their attention to the past experiences of one of the interactants judged relevant to the task at hand. Within an interactional sequence of only a few minutes a large number of share foci can be introduced, attended to, and discarded. The maintenance, modification, and shift of shared foci is one of the basic processes that is a part of all social encounters.

Shared foci can be established via appearance as well as via discourse. A new shared focus can be created by one person pointing to an object with the other person noting and acknowledging the pointing. Of course, if the second person fails to note the pointing of the first person, a shared focus is not established. It is difficult, but not impossible, to establish a shared focus through the universe of touch.

When interactants are reciprocally attentive, socially responsive, and have a shared focus they are implicated with each other in the ongoing present, but these elements of sociation are not sufficient for the production of coordinated action. People must also establish a social objective and produce congruent functional identities to produce units of coordinated action. Coordinated action is structured by social objectives—what *they*, the interacting unit, is attempting to accomplish. Unless a social objective is established persons may act with respect to each other, but they cannot act with each other. Coordinated action is orderly when interactants produce and maintain congruent functional identities. When interactants establish a social objective but produce incongruent functional identities, their action is focused but disorderly. For example, when interactants mutually indicate they are going to plan for a meeting with a representative of the opposition but both of them speak at the same time they have established a social objective, but they produce incongruent functional identities. On the other hand, if one of them speaks and the others listen then they produce congruent functional identities.

In laboratory studies the participants are usually assigned categorical identities and a social objective. When participants accept the assigned categorical identities and social objectives they usually structure their subsequent behavior by activating the functional identities implied by the categorical identities and linking them to a shared focus or series of shared foci. The production of coordinated action requires that both indicate acceptance of the assigned objective and that each participant project future lines of action—functional identities—that are detected by the other.

When we coordinate our actions with another we usually inform each other of what we intend to do with respect to a shared focus through discourse. One can establish a song book as the shared focus by pointing to a song book. But, to establish the social objective of singing a song from the song book together it is necessary to speak of our intentions. Of course, if the act of pointing to a song book is contextualized by a shared past of singing together then the social objective can be established on the basis of a shared past, and intentions need not be put into discourse.

Whenever the social action to be undertaken has any degree of novelty social objectives are nearly always established in discourse. As a consequence participants in laboratory studies almost invariably formulate social objectives via reciprocating speech acts. If the sessions are populated with people who have an extended shared past (friends) then social objectives and congruent functional identities may be established on the basis of elements that are taken for granted.

Once the participants have been positioned and the positioner has withdrawn then the participants typically orient toward each other and mutually validate the assigned objective and categorical identities. They also usually project lines of action and detect the lines of action projected by the other. For example, they often will turn to each other and discuss what it is they are to do. As they converse one indicates she will speak and the other indicates she will listen. When the other indicates she will listen they thereby establish a social objective and congruent functional identities. They do not always establish congruent functional identities immediately. Interactants sometimes interrupt each other or are inattentive. If they are to coordinate their actions, they must be attentive and responsive to each other's action in the ongoing present and to the future projected by the other.

The production of coordinated action requires persons to establish reciprocal attention, social responsiveness, and shared foci plus congruent functional identities and social objectives. The minimal elements of sociation necessary for cooperative action are displayed in Diagram VII.2.

One general type of analysis that can be made of nearly all social encounters is the specification of the symmetry or asymmetry of the attentiveness, responsiveness, and functional identities. In some transactions these elements of sociation are highly asymmetrical, in others they are symmetrical. A degree of reciprocity is always present whenever a unit of social action is

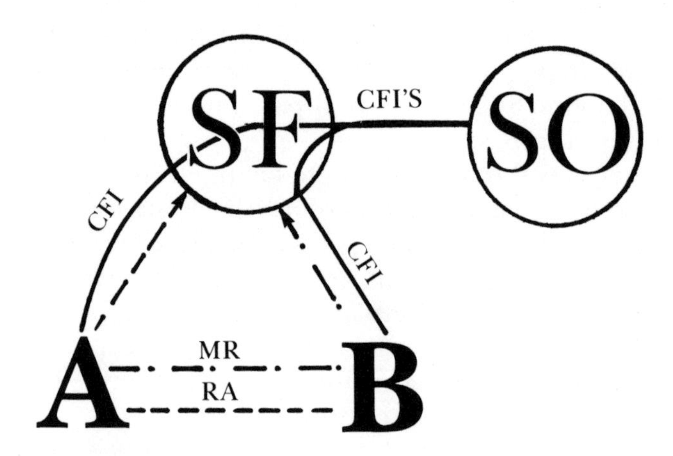

Notes:
RA = Reciprocal Attention
MR = Mutual Responsiveness
CFI = Congruent Functional Identities
SF = Shared Focus
SO = Social Objectives
--- = Attentiveness
—.— = Responsiveness
_____ = Action

Diagram VII. 2. Elements of Sociation Necessary For Dyadic Cooperative Action produced; however, the reciprocity need not be symmetrical. Often it is very asymmetrical. Interactants are symmetrically responsive when each responds to the other with equal intensity. They are asymmetrically responsive when one enthusiastically responds to the acts of the other, while the other person is only minimally responsive to the first person. Perhaps the extreme form of asymmetrical responsiveness is when one person enthusiastically greets another and the other fails to respond. In such transactions one makes a bid for a high level of mutual responsiveness, and all he gets for his trouble is indifference.

In some encounters what is to be achieved and how it is to be achieved is jointly established; in others, one person initiates and the other accepts the program of action offered by the first person. For example, one interactant may refuse to acknowledge or acknowledges but refuses to accept the program of action offered by the other. He may insist that the other follow his lead. If the other consistently accepts the initiations offered by the first person the interaction is asymmetrical; one initiates lines of action and the other aligns his action with the initiations of the first person.

A second general type of analysis that can be completed of almost all encounters is whether or not congruent identities are established and how they are established When a person speaks, through the rhythm of his speech, his body positioning, gaze orientation, and perhaps in the content of his speech he can indicate that his talk is coming to an end and that he anticipates the other will speak. If the other then speaks they maintain congruent functional identities. When congruent functional identities are established and maintained persons align their individual lines of action to create a course of social action that is directed towards the accomplishment of a social objective. Interruptions and other intrusions sometimes render their actions problematic.

The analysis of the elements of sociation displayed in Diagram VII.2. especially the examination of their symmetry versus asymmetry and their congruency versus incongruency, will provide understanding of how elementary units of social action are produced, maintained, transformed, and terminated (Couch, 1986b). The analysis of complex forms of social action, for example, interpersonal negotiations (Sink and Couch, 1986) and interpersonal accounting (Lutfiyya and Miller, 1986), requires concepts that specify more complex elements of sociation.

The sociological analysis of social processes requires concepts that explicitly designate relatedness—elements of sociation. Concepts such as reciprocal acknowledged attention, social responsiveness, shared focus, social objective, congruent identities, (Miller, Hintz, and Couch, 1975), mutually acknowledged untoward act (Lutfiyya and Miller, 1986), mutually recognized differences (Sink and Couch, 1986), solidary responsiveness (Sehested, 1975) and acknowledged announcement (Leichty, 1986) orient analysts to social phenomena.

Once cooperative action is under way interactants usually become intermittently attentive and responsive to each other; they are not continuously attentive and responsive to each other. When the action undertaken by a dyad is novel, then attentiveness to the other and to the shared focus usually is more or less continuous. In either event elements of sociation link persons together; their production creates social bondedness. One of the central tasks when analyzing specimens of social is to note the elements of sociation produced and how the various elements are combined to create different types and levels of social bondedness.

SOCIAL RELATIONSHIPS

Despite the fact that sociological theories are replete with assertions on social relationships and social structure most of the assertions rest upon a very shaky foundation. As Sica (1983) notes, most of the contemporary statements that purport to offer a theory of social relationships and/or social structure are merely reiteration of assertions offered by past masters. Social commentators and social scientists from Plato, through Machiavelli, Jefferson, and Marx, to contemporary theorists have offered one pronouncement after another about the nature of social relationships and their consequences. Few of these assertions are substantiated with sound data.

Laboratory research on social relationships is in a very primitive stage. However, laboratory studies of social relationships promise to become a viable part of the sociological enterprise.

In order for that promise to be fulfilled it will be necessary for the analysts of laboratory generated data on social relationships to adopt and maintain a sociological standpoint while analyzing their data. As it is with the study of social action that requires making activities produced by a dyad the minimum unit of analysis.

In the typical social encounter interactants activate or construct social relationships as well as produce units of social action. In many everyday encounters people activate complex composite social relationships. In contrast, in laboratory sessions, especially those that are cleanly designed and populated with strangers, only the social relationships of positioner-participants plus one other relationship are activated. For example, in a study of bargaining the only social relationship that needs to be activated in addition to that of positioner-participants is an exchange relationship. Nonetheless, the analysis of laboratory generated data on social relationships is, generally speaking, a more complex and intricate undertaking than the analysis of units of social action.

The elements of sociation that compose units of social action are more often explicitly produced than are the elements of sociation that compose social relationships. Many social relationships rest upon a host of taken for granted dimensions that are activated either on the basis of a shared past or by the display and detection of categorical identities communicated in the universe of appearance. Therefore, generally speaking, it is more difficult to specify the elements of sociation that constitute social relationships than it is to specify those that compose forms of social action.

However, that difference is partially counteracted when the laboratory sessions are populated by strangers. If strangers are to activate relationships other than those of strangers, positioner-participant and the one implied by their assigned categorical identities they must either establish additional congruent categorical identities through the universe of appearance, formulate one by producing patterns of interaction, or discuss their relationship. In either event the construction of their relationship is a public process that is available for analysis.

A minimal social relationship is established when interactants consensually assign self and other congruent categorical identities, indicate that they have a shared future which will be at least partly structured by the congruent categorical identities, and mutually indicate a willingness to coordinate their actions within the parameters implied by the social linkages associated with the categorical identities. People with an extended shared past activate complex composite relationships that contain a host of elements of sociation whenever they initiate a social encounter. The specification of the elements of sociation activated when a student and teacher who are also close friends undertake a social enterprise is a complex undertaking. The complexity of such encounters almost defies analysis given our present state of knowledge.

The stark and impoverished relationships of strangers convened in a laboratory within clearly delineated contexts are much more amendable to analysis. Even so, the specification of the elements of sociation that compose a basic social relationship is a complex undertaking. However, the development of empirically grounded theories of social structure is contingent upon the specification of elements of sociation that compose various forms of social relationships, the specification of how different basic forms of social relationships are combined to produce composite social relationships, and the consequences of various relationships.

A few preliminary laboratory studies of social relationships have been completed. Katovich, Weiland, and Couch (1981), Weiland and Couch (1986), and Couch and Weiland (1986) investigated some of the dimensions of the representative relationship. For the most part, these studies focused on the evolution and transformation of the representative relationship under various structural conditions. The elements of sociation that constitute the basic dimensions of the representative relationship are yet to be specified.

Miller (1986a) conducted a study of hypnotic encounters. He conceptualized hypnotic encounters as the prototypical authority relationship. Miller (1986b) also re-analyzed Milgram's studies of obedience in an effort to specify some of the critical elements of the authority relationship. He offers a set of concepts that at least provide a general orienting framework for the analysis of authority relationships generated in laboratories.

Sehested (1975) provides a conceptual framework for the

analysis of solidary relationships. She notes the importance of solidary responsiveness and solidary action for the establishment and maintenance of a solidary relationship. She also notes that solidary relationships rest upon a foundation of a shared past and the significance of asserting and acknowledging collective identities for the re-affirmation of a solidary relationship.

Hardesty (1986b) has specified some of the jointly constructed acts that are necessary for the establishment of a therapeutic relationship. She gives special attention to the fact that it is necessary for the client and therapist to establish a particular mood if a therapeutic relationship is to be activated and the asymmetric nature of the relationship. Katovich (1986) has developed a general scheme for the analysis of the intertwinings of the elements of sociation that are established when interactants become structurally situated. He gives special attention to the temporal dimensions implied by functional identities, categorical identities, interpersonal identities, and instrumental identities when interactants become structurally situated.

Each of the above is but a beginning toward the precise and detailed specification of the elements of sociation that compose the various relationships and their consequences. The analysis of laboratory generated data on these and related issues can provide indepth understanding of social relationships and their consequences. Such knowledge would in turn provide a foundation for the development of empirically grounded theories of social structure.

SUMMARY

The effective use of the laboratory produces simplified and relatively uncontaminated specimens of social action. Video recordings and transcripts offer these specimens so that they can be examined again and again. Despite these advantages, unless analysts of recordings are well armed with concepts that orient them to the social dimensions of the phenomena, little of consequence for sociology will come from these studies.

Recordings of even elementary forms of social action offer analysts complex data to manage. The analyst of video recordings of social action is confronted by an evermoving gestalt of complex phenomena. Unless the phenomena are approached with a conceptual scheme that emphasizes the linkages between persons and the relatedness between dyads, triads, and larger units and their environment, little headway will be made in the analysis of the data.

The overarching objective of analysts is to detect the structure of the processes and the processual structures interactants produce as they align their actions to act upon and react to their environment (Travisano, 1975). In some encounters the reciprocating sets of activities are smoothly produced; other instances of activity display fits and starts. Interactants sometimes misread each other's intentions, sometimes mask their intentions, and, of course, sometimes are incompetent and communicate one thing in one universe of communication and contradictory information in another universe of communication. The fits and starts and the multiple universes of communication complicate the task of analysts. However, often it is the close analysis of disjunctive transactions that provides the most insight into the social processes and social relationships under investigation. This is especially the case when disjunctive segments are compared to smoothly produced segments.

The transactions that are the most difficult to analyze are those produced by persons with a robust shared past who are enthusiastically involved and highly competent. It is almost impossible for an outside observer to decipher either the social processes they produce or the precise nature of the social relationship that contextualizes their action. In contrast, when strangers coordinate their actions in nonroutine situations the elements of sociation that compose the units of social action and social relationships are usually explicitly constructed in sequence. Usually strangers also publicly reaffirm the relationship implied by their assigned categorical identities or explicitly formulate a relationship. Generally speaking, elements of sociation are more readily detectable in social encounters produced by strangers than in those produced by friends.

One of the difficulties in analyzing social processes produced by strangers is that strangers often commit acts that are attention getting but of little relevance; they thereby sometimes confuse the analyst. It is necessary to recognize that interactants sometimes do not know what they are doing. Other times they presume they have activated a consensually agreed to social relationship only to later discover that they disagree. Sometimes they are confused by the situation or confuse themselves. Social order, both from the point of view of those constructing it and from the point of view of an outside observer, is frequently highly problematic. Ambiguity and disorder are inherent features of social life. They, too, must be recognized when making a sociological analysis of laboratory data.

Chapter VIII

Selected Units of Action

The recordings of 8 to 12 episodes of 5 to 6 minutes each plus transcriptions of the recordings present analysts with a tremendous amount of data. The problems created by the quantity of the data sometimes can be alleviated by extracting units of social action from the episodes. A cursory observation of recordings may lead one to think that the action displayed in each episode is continuous; and, in one sense, it is. Whenever people are co-present they continually provide each other with information; that is even the case when they are not aligning their actions, but are merely a part of each other's perceptual field.

It is usually possible to break up the recordings of laboratory encounters into smaller units to make the data more manageable. Sometimes distinctive units of social action can be extracted from the episodes which then can be analyzed while ignoring the rest of the data. The extraction of units of social action for special attention, however, must be sociologically informed and done with caution. The integrity of the social acts must be preserved.

Whenever a researcher extracts units of social action for special analysis he risks overlooking critical data and that may result in a failure to attend to phenomena that might provide an answer to his question. As the analysis proceeds it is advisable for the researcher from time to time to withdraw, adopt a somewhat different standpoint and ask: "Are the transactions that I am extracting the critical ones?"

Several different procedures can be used to extract units of social action from episodes. However, in all cases it is the accomplishments of the dyad or triad that must be used to delineate the beginning and ending of each extracted unit of social action. The bracketing of each unit to be extracted is made by noting key transactions between the interactants. Four general procedures have been used to extract units of social action from the recorded episodes. They are: (1) dividing each episode into its opening, middle, and ending; (2) analyzing only those transactions framed by the assigned categorical identities; (3) extracting specific forms of social activity from each episode; and (4) selecting transactions that transforms either the nature of the social action, their relationship, or their social objective. Whenever any of these procedures are used it is necessary for the researcher to reexamine the total recorded episodes from time to time to make certain that critical transactions are not overlooked.

TEMPORAL STAGES

All units of cooperative action contain three distinctive stages—openings, middles, and endings. Some simple forms of social activity, for example, greetings by passerbys and mutual accommodative encounters do not contain a middle. These encounters do not contain a shared focus or social objective. Those who construct them are merely reciprocally attentive and socially responsive. However, the recordings of episodes produced within a laboratory nearly always contain openings, middles and endings.

The division of an episode into its opening, middle, and ending cannot be made on the basis of clock time. The division must be made on the basis of the accomplishments of the interactants. The opening stage includes those transactions that begin when two persons make social contact and ends when they have established congruent identities that are linked to a social objective. The middle of the encounter begins when a social objective is established and concludes when the interactants begin disaffiliating from each other. Endings begin when the interactants move to disaffiliate and conclude when co-presence is destroyed. After recorded episodes have been divided on this basis the openings and the endings can then be subjected to a detailed analysis. If the episodes are more than a minute or so in duration the middles will still retain a wealth of data.

Participants in laboratory studies construct an opening with the positioner when they appear to take part in the study. After they have been assigned their categorical identities and a social objective they must reopen or functionally situate themselves with each other to accomplish their assigned tasks. They readily accomplish this in most contexts by activating congruent functional identities that are consistent with their assigned categorical identities and linked to the social objective they have been assigned. In most instances participants will functionally situate themselves within a few seconds after positioner leaves the room. Furthermore, in most contexts the transactions produced by the participants as they turn their attention from the positioner and functionally situate themselves are highly uniform.

In most cases how the participants become functionally situated will differ by context. When that is the case, a thorough examination of how the participants reopen and become functionally situated within the contexts they have been provided can be revealing. In the study of representative relationships based upon early versus late differentiation of the partisan groups, the members of the two sets of triads situated themselves very differently when they directed their efforts to their assigned task. In the triads that were differentiated before they started planning the two constituents focused their attention on the person designated as the representative as soon as the positioner left the room. In the triads not differentiated prior to planning no one served as the focal point. The members of these triads became situated by giving intermittent attention to each other as they gave primary attention to the information we had given them. The members of these two sets of triads functionally situated themselves in two very distinctive ways; or, they activated two different types of relationships.

In the study of parental relationships how the parent and child functionally situated themselves was associated with the gender of the parent. In those dyads composed of a mother and child, the mother nearly always initiated the openings; in contrast, in those dyads composed of a father and child, the child usually initiated the openings and had his initiation validated by the father.

During the opening stages of an encounter interactants usually establish or reaffirm their relationship. Consequently, openings often contains elements of sociation that establish relationships that frame subsequent actions. In many instances laboratory participants become both functionally and structurally situated almost immediately after they have received their instructions and the positioner has left the room.

In some studies, especially those studies composed of multiepisode sessions, when participants move from one episode to the next they must establish or reaffirm their relationship. For example, when representatives of groups leave their respective groups to meet with the representative of the opposing group it is necessary for them to activate a relationship in order to become become structurally and functionally situated when they convene to conduct intergroup negotiations. In the studies we have conducted the two negotiators were assigned the categorical identity of representative and the social objective of negotiating with each other, but when they convened for the intergroup negotiation sessions it was still necessary for them to functionally situate themselves as representatives and negotiators before an intergroup negotiation session could occur.

When we first began these studies we presumed that whenever participants had been assigned categorical identities they would activate functional identities consistent with their assigned categorical identities. However, as we studied these recordings it became apparent that in some cases these participants did not become structurally situated was intergroup negotiators. In some of the intergroup meetings very little intergroup negotiations was completed. All representatives constructed a functional opening as interactants when they convened for the intergroup negotiation sessions, but some failed to structurally situate themselves as representatives with competing interests.

In most of these episodes the two representatives quickly situated themselves as representatives and turned to the task of negotiating their differences. However, in a few cases the categorical identity of the representative of the partisan group was challenged by the dean. One dean, for example, asked the representative to specify just what group it was that she represented. Another wanted to know how the committee had been elected and how she, the representative, has been selected. These deans rendered the categorical identity of the representatives of the partisan groups problematic; and, for a moment at least, prevented the two of them from becoming structurally situated as negotiators. Before intergroup negotiation could proceed it was necessary for the representative of the partisan group to entice the dean to acknowledge her categorical identity. Only after the relevant categorical identities have been mutually acknowledged could intergroup negotiations proceed. In one case when the dean quizzed the representative of the partisan group about how many students she represented, the partisan group representative turned the tables and asked the dean how many students he, the dean, represented.

The systematic analysis of the opening moments of social encounters will often reveal many dimensions of social encounters that usually are taken for granted. Interactants most often explicitly direct their efforts toward the activation and negotiation of their social relationship in the early moments of encounters. The social relationship activated during those earlier moments usually establish the parameters for the encounter that contextualizes and structures subsequent activities of the interactants. The detailed study of openings holds considerable promise for advancing our understanding of social order—how it is established, maintained, and transformed.

The mere fact that persons initiate a social encounter and become functionally situated as interactors does not automatically result in them becoming structurally situated. Even when persons meet for the explicit purpose of negotiating a settlement of a strike in the day-to-day world they sometimes fail to become structurally situated as intergroup negotiators. Many times representatives of competing groups meet to negotiate mutually recognized differences, become angry with one another, and fail to become structurally situated as negotiators. To become structurally situated as intergroup negotiators requires the interactants to mutually activate congruent functional of negotiators as well as consensual categorical identities of representatives (Katovich, 1986).

Endings, especially closings (Leichty, 1986), are also a very fruitful research site. When people construct a social closing they explicitly attend to their relationship. During social closings a series of transactions are produced by interactants that specify and affirm the nature of their relationship.

Many of the episodes within the laboratory are terminated by the positioners interjecting themselves. The analysis of those terminations is usually not fruitful. These terminations are usually brought about by the participants simply discontinuing to attend to each other and becoming attentive and responsive to the positioner. However, in some studies the episodes are terminated by the participants constructing a social closing. When that is the case these endings can be extracted and analyzed as distinctive units of social action.

When social closings are extracted it is necessary to specify the criteria for the beginning of the closing and its termination. Two somewhat different criteria can be used to specify the beginning of a closing. One might use the criterion of an acknowledged announcement (Leichty, 1986). Then one would extract from the recordings and transcriptions the transactions that begin when the interactants produce reciprocating acts whereby they mutually indicate they—the two of them—recognize that they are about to terminate the encounter. An alternative criterion for the specification of the beginning of a closing is when one of the interactants indicates the encounter is about to be terminated and it is judged that the other noted the indication whether or not he acknowledged it. If the second criteria is used, then if one person said something like, "Our time is about up" that remark would mark the beginning of the closing even if the other completely ignored the assertion, but in the judgment of the analyst the other interactant had noted and understood the comment.

Whichever criterion is used, then all activity from the beginning of the closing to the destruction of copresence would be extracted from the episodes and examined to specify how the participants brought their encounter to an end.

Generally speaking, it is at the beginning and ending of social encounters that relationship centered interaction is most salient. It is when we greet and leave each other that we are most likely to do "relationship work." The detailed study of openings and closings promises to yield considerable understanding of the nature of the many types of social relationships and their consequences (Miller, Hintz, and Couch, 1975; Katovich, 1986; Hardesty, 1986b; Leichty, 1986).

PARING OFF IRRELEVANT TRANSACTIONS

Not all of the activities of laboratory participants are framed by the context, identities and objectives assigned. Some of the transactions are framed by the identities and objectives which they activate that locate them outside of those assigned to them by their positioner. For example, in the accounting sessions that followed the meetings of representatives in studies of intergroup negotiations the participants often activated several identities other than that of members of a partisan group. That most commonly occurred in those groups wherein the constitutes became alienated from their representatives. Some of these groups activated identities based on their university classification, their major field of study and/or classes they were taking shortly after the representative had completed her report of what had transpired in the intergroup negotiation session. When identities of that sort were activated the participants then addressed such issues as how they came to take part in the study, the purpose of the study, the nature of classes they are enrolled in, and how long they have been attending the university.

When we first analyzed the transactions between the representatives and their constituents in the accounting episodes following the meeting of the groups' representatives with the opposition we attempted to code all activity produced during those episodes. In one study we compared the transactions in the accounting episodes where the constituents had an independent source of information with the episodes where the constituents had to rely on their representative's report to acquire information about what had occurred in his meeting with the opposition (Katovich, Weiland and Couch, 1981).

In some of the groups where constituents did not receive an independent report of what happened, the accounting episodes simply consisted of the representative giving a report and the constituents passively accepting it. In many of these episodes the report of the representative was followed by sticky silence which in turn was followed by one of the participants introducing a topic that was not linked to their partisan position, to the intergroup negotiations, or to the identities assigned to them.

In this study one of our central concern was specifying if the constituents "had a say" during the accounting episode. The first criterion used for "having a say" was that a person made an assessment of something and had that assessment accepted or modified by another member of the triad. Each recording and transcript was searched for transactions wherein one person made an explicit assessment and another member of the triad attended to the assessment offered.

When these data were approached in this manner it quickly became apparent that the constituents in the groups without an independent source of information less frequently had a say. Many of the constituents offered assessments, but usually these assessments were ignored or deflected by the representative and the other constituent. In contrast, in the groups that had an independent source of information most of the assessments offered by one or both constituents were acknowledged and either accepted or elaborated upon by another member of the triad. The differences between the two sets of episodes were quite distinct.

However, as we continued our analysis we realized that a wide range of shared foci were established. Some of the transactions focused on what had occurred in the intergroup negotiation meetings, others established the purpose of the study as the shared focus, and a few groups discussed the people conducting study. We then noted that when a constituent in the groups that did not have an independent source of information made an assessment of the study, those running the study, classes at the university, or any other topic not directly linked to the intergroup negotiation meeting, his assessment was usually acknowledged and attended to by at least one other member of the triad. In contrast, when a constituent in those same groups made an assessment of what had transpired in the intergroup negotiations his assessment was nearly always ignored, or if not ignored, deflected by the representative changing the topic.

We then reformulated our criterion for "having a say" and reanalyzed the data. This time we established the criterion for "having a say" as making a characterization of what happened in the intergroup negotiation session and having that statement accepted or modified by another member of the triad. The differences between the two conditions were more dramatic than when the analysis was based on all of the assessments made.

When the analysis was restricted to those topics framed by the identities of representative and constituent the differences between the two comparison groups were not only more distinctive but of greater theoretical significance. Whenever the members of those triads wherein the constituents did not have an independent source of information interacted as representatives and constituents and addressed past events relevant to their partisan position those representatives with a monopoly of knowledge almost completely dominated the interaction. Yet when members of these same triads activated other identities, such as university student, they usually interacted as equals.

In the analysis of many episodes attention can be restricted to those transactions directly linked to the assigned identities and objectives, while ignoring all transactions not framed by their assigned identities. The paring off of the other transactions, however, must be done with caution. When the paring off can be theoretically justified, it is a procedure that sometimes will render the data more manageable, and yield findings of greater theoretical significance than if all the transactions are analyzed.

SELECTED FORMS OF ACTION

Within nearly all episodes of more than a minute or so duration, the interactants construct a number of different forms of social action. Within a span of a few minutes a given dyad may negotiate, resituate themselves, verbally conflict, bargain, and construct an aborted closing. When a given set of recordings contain a number of transactions of a particular type, than those transactions can be extracted from the recordings and analyzed. The elements and structure of interpersonal negotiations (Sink and Couch, 1986) and interpersonal accounting (Lutfiyya and Miller, 1986) were isolated in this manner.

Before undertaking this type of analysis it is necessary to formulate a tentative set of criteria of what constitutes a given form of social action. After the tentative criteria have been formulated then the recordings and transcriptions are searched for instances of that form of social action. Once the original search has been made, it will usually become apparent that the original criteria were not adequate. Then the criteria are reformulated and the recordings and transcripts are searched again for instances of the form of social action under investigation. This procedure, perhaps more than any other, involves continual reformulation of the problem and reconceptualization of the phenomena.

Lutfiyya and Miller first searched a set of recordings and transcriptions for "accounts." Prior studies of accounts (Scott and Lyman, 1968; Hewitt and Stokes, 1973; Tedeschi and Reiss, 1980) provided the guidelines for the first selection of the units of social to be analyzed. Then the recordings and transcriptions were searched for accounts.

The question that was addressed in this study was somewhat different than that of earlier studies of accounts. Namely, the intent was to detect the elements of sociation that constitute interpersonal accounting. Therefore, the recordings and transcripts were searched once again to note the responses of the other to whom an account was directed. The accounting process is not completed until the account is accepted by another.

As the researchers worked with the data it became apparent that the acts immediately preceding the account were significant. That led to a reconceptualization of the accounting process. The beginning of the accounting process was then designated as occurring when a "mutually recognized untoward act has been committed." Subsequently the data were researched once again for all transactions containing a mutually recognized untoward act.

The beginnings of the final set of transactions were delineated by a mutually recognized untoward act and the endings were delineated by either the acceptance of an offered account or when it was judged an account would not be offered. After these transactions had been extracted then the accounts offered in various contexts were analyzed.

The original question that was addressed in the research that resulted in the specification of the elements and structure or interpersonal negotiations was: How do triads achieve a unified standpoint? As the analysis proceeded it became apparent that proposals and counter proposals were critical transactions. It then became apparent that the proposals and counter proposals were framed by both a mutually recognized difference among the interactants and a mutual concern with resolving their differences. The original question of how does a unified standpoint become established when there are differences was changed to: What elements of sociation must interactants produce to resolve their differences? That question was further refined to: Is there a sequential order in the production of the elements of sociation that result in the resolution of differences?

Further study of the recordings and transcriptions revealed that sometimes the establishment of mutually recognized differences was followed by proposals and counter proposals and sometimes it was not. Then, all transactions that established a mutually recognized difference were isolated. The transactions that occurred subsequent to the establishment of a mutually recognized difference were extracted. Then, those sets of transactions that resulted in the formation of a consensual position were compared with those that did not.

As the analysis proceeded we again reformulated our question. The final question that framed our analysis was: What are the elements and structure of interpersonal negotiations?

The social act that was originally the primary focus of our attention, the display of a consensual standpoint toward an issue, was refined into three elements of sociation—the formation of agreements, the forging of social commitments, and the ending of negotiations.

When studies of this type are undertaken there is an almost continual interplay between the formulation of the question, the units of social action attended to, and the explanation of the phenomena under investigation. As one moves toward achieving an explanation, the original question is modified; as the question is modified some of the data originally thought relevant are no longer relevant, and data not originally attended to often become critical.

TRANSFORMATIONS

People frequently transform the nature of their relatedness within social encounters. On occasion a friendly game of cards transforms into a heated argument. Competitors sometimes become combatants. Lovers sometimes become enemies; authorities are sometimes deposed by their subordinates. Many of these transformations occur incrementally; others cataclysmically. Participants in laboratory studies seldom cataclysmically transform their relatedness. In most sessions they establish and sustain the relationships implied by the contexts and identifies assigned to them. However, on some occasions they do transform their relationships. When that occurs the systematic analysis of the transformations can be very fruitful.

In order for people to transform their relationship they must publicly inform each other of changes in how they locate themselves with respect to each other. The transformation is completed when they achieve consensus on their new form of relatedness. These units of social action can be extracted by noting when one of the interactants makes a bid for changing the nature of their relationship and all subsequent transactions until a new relationship is consensually established or until the original relationship is reaffirmed.

It is far more difficult to isolate the elements of sociation that constitute a social relationship by comparing two sets of nonchanging relationships than by analyzing transformations from one type of social relationship to another type. The reason for that is that in order for strangers to change their relationship in a short period of time it is usually necessary for them to explicitly make the nature of their relatedness their shared focus. In contrast, to maintain an established relationship all that is necessary is for the interactants to continue to act in the same manner as they have been acting.

The examination of the transactions between representatives and their constituents in the accounting episodes that follow the intergroup negotiations allowed us to acquire some knowledge of the representative relationship. The structure of all of these groups underwent some modification when the representative and constituents reconvened following the intergroup negotiating sessions. In some of the groups the transformations of the relatedness between the participants were profound. It was by comparing those groups in which major transformations occurred with groups that maintained the assigned relationship that we have been able to specify some of the elements of sociation that constitute the representative relationship (Katovich, Weiland and Couch, 1981, Weiland and Couch, 1986, Couch and Weiland, 1986).

The study of transformational processes usually is more effective if some of the groups under analysis transform and others do not. Then the transactions that are produced within those groups that undergo a transformation can be compared with those of groups that do not transform. Researchers can then determine the transactions that are critical for bringing about the transformation and which ones are incidental to the transformation.

SUMMARY

Unless a researcher restricts his analysis to units of social action of short duration he is likely to find himself attempting to attend to so much data that it is impossible to complete the analysis. One of the burdens of a sociological analyst of video recordings is that he must maintain a rather broad scope of attention while analyzing data. At the minimum he has to attend to the actions of two persons and the actions they take toward some third object. Furthermore, to generate data that can be brought to bear on many sociological questions it is necessary to allow the participants to interact for several minutes. Even when studies are parsimoniously designed the episodes usually endure for at least a few minutes. Consequently, the laboratory researcher when analyzing video recordings is confronted with so much data that he often has difficulty managing it unless he pushes some of the data aside so that he can focus his attention on the data critical to his question.

The management of the data can sometimes be facilitated by selecting out units of social action that are especially critical. The selection of these smaller units of social action cannot be made on the basis of clock time. Analysts must establish sociological criteria for extracting the units of action to be examined. Only then can these select units of social action be analyzed while ignoring other segments of the recordings and transcriptions.

All research endeavors are focused acts. It is necessary to be selective when attending to data. The danger of extracting units of social action from recordings and transcriptions is that focused attention is also a form of selective blindness. Sometimes by narrowly focusing one's attention, the data necessary to answer the question posed are excluded. It is often necessary to reformulate the question and establish new criteria for the selection of the transactions to be extracted. Then the recordings and transcriptions data can be re-examined. Researchers must adopt a standpoint and focus their attention, but at the same time it is necessary for them to recognize that they are examining the data from a distinctive standpoint and that they have thereby narrowed their focus of attention.

Chapter IX

Analyzing Triadic Processes

Many sociological questions can be addressed by studying dyadic processes. However, some social processes and relationships only appear in triads and larger units. The study of coalitions, interpersonal mediation and three-tiered authority structures requires the analysis of processes produced by three or more people. When the units of analysis are processes produced by a triad instead of a dyad there is an increase of only 50 percent in the number of people, but, the complexity of the social processes increases several fold.

When members of a dyad coordinate their actions they relate by each attending and responding to the other as the two of them attend to and act toward a shared focus. In contrast, when members of a triad coordinate their actions, A and B are reciprocally attentive and socially responsive; A and C are reciprocally attentive and socially responsive; B and C are reciprocally attentive and socially responsive as the three of them attend to and act toward a shared focus. Dyadic cooperative action is composed of three parts—the two people and their shared focus. Three lines of connectedness link all three parts. Triadic cooperative behavior is composed of four parts—the three people and their shared focus. It requires six lines of connectedness to link all four parts.

It is difficult for a person to be simultaneously attentive and responsive to two other persons and a shared focus. Therefore it is much more difficult for a triad to coordinate its action than it is for a dyad. The difficulties of a researcher attempting to analyze triadic processes are even greater than those of a member of a triad. Unless, of course, the researcher has the advantage of recordings and transcriptions of the transactions.

Human interaction is essentially a dyadic phenomenon; it is difficult for three people to be simultaneously attentive and responsive to each other. Consequently within triadic encounters one person often becomes the focal point while the other two are primarily attentive and responsive to the focal person and relatively indifferent to each other. Often, the focal person attends to the other two by "lumping" them together as a unit. For example, during a triadic conversation at any moment a common condition is for one to speak while the other two listen. When that occurs the speaker either serially notes the attentiveness of the listeners by glancing from one to the other or treats the two of them as a unit. Then when one of the listeners begins to speak the other two are altercast as listeners.

Triadic interaction is further confounded by the temporal structures that inform and guide the behavior of the members of the triad (Molseed, 1986). A must note the projected futures of both B and C; B must note the projected futures of both A and C; and C must note the projected futures of both A and B as they coordinate their actions to achieve social objectives. In contrast, dyadic interactants only need to note each other's projected future.

Simmel (1950) offered a framework for the analysis of triadic relationships. However, his framework is a point in time approach that focuses on relationships; he implies processes but he does not provide a framework for the examination of triadic processes. For example, he notes that mediation can only occur in triads or larger groups, but does not offer any guidelines for the study of the processes of mediation. The only triadic processes given attention by Simmel are transformations of the structure of triads. Transformations are critical, but processes in addition to the transformations of structures also occur in triads. Simmel directed attention to triadic relationships, but not all the activity produced by triads is relationship focused. Most triadic action, like most dyadic action, is framed by a stable relationship and is focused on events and objects external to the triad.

The complex combinations of relationships possible within

triads and the fact that human beings can simultaneously communicate through touch, appearance, and discourse makes the analysis of triadic processes difficult. The analyst of triadic activity is confronted with a severe challenge. It is a challenge that is almost impossible to meet without the benefit of recordings *and* transcriptions. It is possible to make a rather thorough analysis of simple and short dyadic encounters without transcriptions. But, it is almost, if not totally, impossible to make an adequate analysis of simple 3 minute triadic encounters without both transcriptions and recordings.

TREATING THE TRIAD AS A DYAD

For some purposes it is possible to conceptualize the transactions within groups of three as if they were produced by a dyad; or analyze triadic encounters as if they were dyadic encounters. This method of rendering the data more manageable is only appropriate when the phenomena under investigation are processes that can be constructed by a dyad. When this procedure is employed the analyst ignores the fact there are three people present and focuses on the transactions produced by two people in the presence of a third person.

This procedure was followed in the study that isolated the elements and structure of interpersonal negotiations (Sink and Couch, 1986). The data set consisted of recordings of three persons planning for an intergroup negotiation session. These groups had the tasks of formulating their program of action for the forthcoming meeting and selecting their group's representative. All three members of these took part in the discussions that centered on these two issues. Yet nearly all of the transactions were dyadic. Two persons negotiated an issue at any given moment. The interaction was essentially dyadic. On occasions two members of a triad formed a coalition against the third person. These transactions were treated as if they were between two persons.

Several triadic processes consist of a series of dyadic transactions wherein two people actively relate to one another while the third person, for the moment, is a bystander. For example, bargaining in the context of a unilateral monopoly requires at the minimum three parties—one party with a monopoly on a good desired by at least two other parties. When more than one potential buyer is present the seller with a monopoly will usually bargain serially with the other two. Each transaction between the seller and one of the potential buyers is contextualized by the presence of the other potential buyer. Yet, each bargaining sequence is produced by a dyad. The third party may intrude upon the two who are bargaining and abort the offer and counter offer sequence between the other two, but it is for all practical purposes impossible for a triad to simultaneously maintain two episodes of bargaining. Or course when one party has a monopoly he can, if he so chooses, transform the encounter into an auction. If the encounter is transformed into an auction, then all three parties are simultaneously active participants.

The simplification of triadic transactions by analyzing them as if they were dyadic is a viable procedure only when the form of social action under investigation is one that can be constructed by a dyad. This procedure cannot be used if the issue in question is coalition formation, intragroup mediation, or other processes distinctive to triads.

TRIADIC COORDINATION

Members of a triad must establish a focus shared, have three way agreement on their social objective, more or less continuously monitor each other, be responsive to each other, and project future lines of action that are detected by the other two in order to coordinate their activities. The production of triadic coordinated action requires that all of the linkages displayed in Diagram IX.1. be established. It is difficult for human beings to simultaneously attend to such complex linkages and to be triadically responsive to all at the same time.

One consequence is that triadic action is more often explicitly programmed and based on a division of labor than is dyadic action. For example, one person might say, "You two lift the box and I'll put the brick underneath." Such statements offer an explicit program and a division of labor. Not all coordinated efforts by triads include a division of labor. Some coordinated actions of triads are achieved by all acting in unison and producing parallel lines of action. For example, when a trio sings in unison all produce more or less identical lines of action that fit together into a course of social action.

Coordination is often based on turn taking. Turn taking is somewhat problematic in dyadic interaction; it is more problematic in triads. Interruptions and other intrusions are more common in triadic interaction than in dyadic interaction. When the participants are highly involved in a novel task their interaction often is disjointed as they flit from topic to topic and step on each other's lines. In some instances it is almost impossible to specify the sequence of social events that are produced.

One way of making triadic data more manageable is to focus attention on only two persons at a time. The recordings and transcriptions are approached by first attending to the trans-

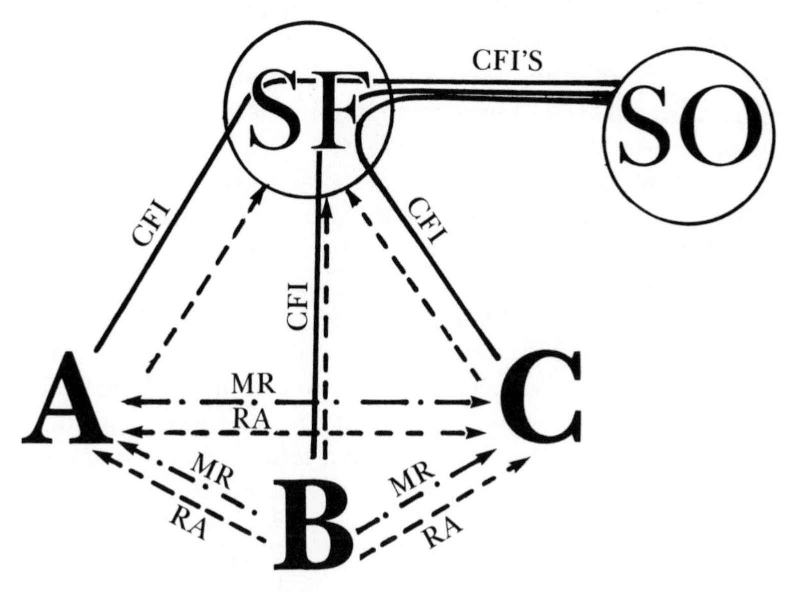

Notes:
RA = Reciprocal Attention
MR = Mutual Responsiveness
CFI = Congruent Functional Identity
SF = Shared Focus
SO = Social Objective
--- = Attentiveness
—.— = Responsiveness
_____ = Action

Diagram IX. 1. Elements of Sociation Necessary For Triadic Cooperative Action

actions between A and B, then again by focusing on the transactions between A and C; and a third time by noting the transactions between B and C. This procedure requires making three "sweeps" through the data.

There is the danger of over concretizing the data with this procedure. Many triadic processes are not merely three sets of dyadic processes. Some have a wholeness on the triadic level. To complete the analysis of those processes the analyst must simulatneously note the actions of all three members of the triad and how the actions of all three fit together.

The transactions within triadic encounters are often a complex intermixture of dyadic and triadic acts. This was often the case in the planning and accounting sessions of the partisan groups of our studies of intergroup negotiations. A common occurrence was for one person to make a suggestion of what to do with one other person responding while the third person passively observed. These transactions were essentially dyadic; or those of a dyad with an audience.

There were other transactions that were triadic in nature. One of the more common triadic transactions in the studies of intergroup negotiations was the production of three-way solidary responsiveness within the partisan groups (Sehested, 1975). An example of this type of transaction is when one person makes a joking characterization of the opposition and all three laugh in unison. The three-way laughter informs all that they all share the same standpoint toward the opposition. On other occasions one person made a joking characterization of the situation and only the person who made the statement and one of the others laughed. In these cases a unit of dyadic solidarity was produced, but not triadic solidarity. Both instances of dyadic and triadic solidarity within the triads must be noted in order to complete an analysis of the level of solidarity produced in groups. On some occasions a triad will produce a robust three-way solidarity; on other occasions two members will establish a robust dyadic solidarity that does not include the third party.

The procedure of focusing in turn on the transactions between each of the three dyads that constitute a triad sometimes facilitates the detection of processes that might otherwise go unnoticed. For example, in our preliminary analysis of the transactions between the boss and his workers of the authority study we gave little attention to the transactions between the two workers. In fact, we were relatively unaware of them. Nearly all of the transactions were between the boss and one worker at a time; on occasions the boss issued directives to the two of them. One, for example, stated, "If you guys don't start working faster, I'm going to go broke." There seemed to be very little transpiring between the workers.

Later we focused our attention on the two workers while ignoring the transactions between the boss and the workers. Most of the interaction between the two workers was subtle, however it was a very rich field of investigation. In many of the sessions, especially those with nonexpert bosses, an "underground" relationship was established between the workers. They rather routinely kept "in touch" with each other while they worked on their assigned tasks and responded to the directives of their boss. They seldom spoke to each other; nearly all of their discourse was either in response to the boss's statements or queries directed to the boss. However, interlaced with this discourse activity were a complex set of transactions between the workers as they made eye contact, exchanged knowing smiles, nodded, winked, and shrugged shoulders. Occasionally, they would make a cryptic comment about the context, but most of their interaction was in the universes of touch and appearance.

This form of interaction between the workers was most common in those sessions where bosses had no more information about how to complete the task than the workers. In those sessions where the bosses were provided with more information than was given to the workers the workers tended to remain "atomized" throughout the sessions. This difference might not have been detected had we not explicitly focused our attention on the transactions between the two workers while actively ignoring the transactions between the boss and the workers.

After the transactions between members of each of the three dyads within a triad have been completed it is then necessary to step back and observe the transactions on a triadic level. Many of the social events produced by the three interactants are qualitatively different from dyadic transactions. For example, in the authority study the transactions between the two workers were significant in their own right, but they acquired another dimension of significance when the transactions between the two workers are noted by the boss. On several occasions the boss noted the exchange of knowing smiles between the workers, but none of the bosses made any comment about them. Yet his awareness that his workers were in touch with each other about his incompetence had an impact on his behavior toward them.

TRANSFORMATION OF TRIADIC STRUCTURES

The inherent complexity of triadic action renders their internal relationships more problematic than dyadic relationships. The nature and intensity of the several axes of relatedness between three interactants rather continually change as members of triads accomplish social objectives (Molseed, 1987). Many of these shifts modify the position of one or more members of the triad. Within triads individuals are almost routinely elevated, demoted, excluded, and incorporated as triads accomplish objectives. Some of these shifts occur very gradually as, for example, when two members of a triad slowly become more responsive to each other and less responsive to the third person. On other occasions the structure of a triad is radically transformed in a few seconds.

Generally speaking transformations of relationships within a laboratory context are far more common within triadic encounters than within dyadic encounters. This is especially the case when the sessions contain more than one episode. Sometimes the transformations of triadic relationships are cataclysmic. Cataclysmic transformations of dyadic relationships are not unknown. On occasion lovers have become enemies; and, if the movies and television shows are to be believed, on occasion enemies become lovers. But, in general, dyadic structures have greater constancy than do triadic structures; and that seems to be especially the case for dyads and triads convened in a laboratory.

In many instances the critical transactions that precede a transformation in the structure of triad are those between two members of a triad when the shared focus is the third person. In our studies of the representative relationship the two persons who had been constituents on several occasions formed a coalition and then deposed their representative during the accounting sessions (Couch and Weiland, 1986). On other occasions during the planning sessions an implicit coalition was formed as two members of a triad attended and responded to each other's suggestions while ignoring the proposals of the third member. That frequently was followed by the third member becoming a passive bystander.

Some of the more dramatic transformations that we have observed have been those that occur within a triad when a representative returned to her group to report the outcome of her meeting with the opposition. In all cases when the representative reconvened with her constituents following an intergroup negotiation episode the representative was the focal person for at least the opening moments. The two constituents typically focused their attention on the representative and she acted toward them as a unit and informed them about the outcome of the intergroup negotiations. In many instances the representative remained the focal point and the dominant person. In other instances she remained the focal point for a short time but then some of the constituents became angry at their representative. Sometimes, they then acted in unison toward her to stigmatize her (Couch and Weiland, 1986).

On occasion the relationship was transformed in a manner of a few seconds. In one case shortly after the representative began her report the facial expressions of the constituents informed the representative that they were displeased with her performance. Then the two constituents made eye contact and one blurted, "Nothing much got accomplished!" The other constituent agreed with, "Obviously!" They then oriented toward each other and derisively laughed. One queried the other with "what are we to do?" The two constituents then began planning for the next meeting while actively ignoring their representative. The representative had been deposed. She made two half-hearted efforts to participate in the planning but her comments were rebuffed. She then bowed her head and examined her fingernails. Her position had changed from being the focal person of the interaction to that of an outcast.

Not all transformations are that dramatic nor are that quickly accomplished. In some cases only one of the constituents explicitly expressed displeasure with the representative's performance. In none of the cases that we have analyzed did the representative lose her focal position when she was attacked by a single constituent. She had served as the group's representative and had more information than the constituents. These factors allowed the representatives to withstand an attack from a single member. In the cases we have observed the representative was only deposed when the two constituents acted in unison to discredit her. Apparently, when one member of the triad has been differentiated and has served as the focal point it requires a coalition of two or more to depose her if she makes an effort to retain her special position.

In many of those triads that did not undergo a radical transformation the two constituents did not become reciprocally attentive and mutually responsive. They remained primarily oriented toward the representative. Many of these constituents merely became unresponsive to their representative. They did not acknowledge nor accept her statements. In these groups the representative while giving her report noted the displeasure of her constituents and some of them became unsure of themselves. Sometimes all three became ill-at-ease. The structure of these triads changed, but the changes were more subtle and less dramatic then when the constituents formed a coalition and acted in unison to stigmatize and/or depose their representative.

To provide an explanation of these and other transformations it is necessary to note the transactions between all three members. These transactions can be very complex. For example, in one triad one of the constituents leveled a bitter attack on the representative and looked toward the other constituent. The other constituent looked away. The representative noted this aborted transaction between the two constituents. She then became firm in resisting the attack of the unhappy constituent. After she had disposed of the criticisms of the attacking constituent she engaged the other constituent in a pleasant conversation and actively ignored the unhappy constituent. In this instance, the attacking constituent became a marginal member of the triad.

Perhaps the most effective procedure for the analysis of the transformations of the structure of triads is to compare the transactions that result in transformations of the relationships within triads with the transactions in other triads where the same issue is addressed but no transformation of the relationships occurs. In the case of representative relationships non-verbal transactions between the two constituents were often critical. The non-verbal transactions in the form of eye contact, fleeting smiles, aggressive stares, shrugs, etc. established a foundation for the constituents to speak in unison against their representative. Unless a researcher deliberately focuses his attention on these subtle transactions they can easily be overlooked.

When analyzing transformations of this type it is necessary to simultaneously examine what is transpiring between the representative and the constituents, what is transpiring between the constituents and how the constituents act in unison toward their representative. It is the total intermixture of the activities that accounts for the transformation, not acts of individuals, nor solely the acts of a dyad within a triad.

Cataclysmic transformations are inherently intriguing. Their dramatic nature captures our attention. It is very easy to become enthralled with the dramatic transactions and ignore the more routine transformations. Both the exciting and the routine transformations have to be attended to in order to isolate the elements of sociation that provide an explanation of how transformations are accomplished. When the one who has served as the group's representative is criticized by one constituent and the other constituent sits there like a lump on a log the events are far less exciting than when both constituents snipe at their representative. Yet, the careful study of transactions like the former one can be as revealing as the study of the more dramatic affairs.

Changes and transformations of the structures of triads offer students of social structure a rich field of investigation. The analysis of the destruction, transformation, and construction of social relationships promises to generate considerable knowledge of the basic dimensions of social structures. Many different types of relationships that are the basic infrastructure of complex social systems can be elucidated by the study of the transformations of the structures of triads.

CONCLUSIONS

One of the primary reasons for conducting laboratory studies of social processes is to render the data more manageable. One procedure for simplifying the data is to conduct studies of dyadic encounters. However, to address some sociological questions it is necessary to compose units of three persons. To investigate coalition formation, intragroup mediation and three tiered structures the minimal unit of analysis has to be the triad. These phenomena cannot be investigated when the focus of attention is limited to dyadic interaction. The transactions produced by triads provide social scientists with a rich field of investigation, a field of study that as yet is relatively untapped. Through the study of triadic transactions social scientists can greatly expand our understanding of complex social phenomena.

It is slightly more difficult to design and run laboratory studies of triads than of dyads. It is infinitely more difficult to complete the analysis of triadic encounters than it is to analyze dyadic transactions. But, the laboratory and video technology provide a means for the systematic and detailed analysis of triadic encounters, an effort that is almost, if not totally, impossible to complete outside of the laboratory and without recording technology.

A vast number of sociological issues can be addressed by attending to triadic encounters. It may be premature to attempt studies of units larger than triads in the laboratory. However, several exciting and novel lines of investigation await those willing to expend the time and effort to study larger groups. For example, the pentad offers many possibilities. One of which is that within a pentad, a minority of two can confront a majority of three. These and many other complex encounters can be elicited in the laboratory and would provide those foolhardy enough to undertake them exceedingly rich data.

Chapter X

Sequences, Forms, and Quantities

Some social scientists equate the analysis of sociological data with quantification and the computation of algebraic formulae (Blalock, 1960; Babbie, 1973). That equation is one of the greatest misfortunes to fall upon social science. The analysis of social phenomena entails far more than noting frequencies and computing correlations. At the minimum, it requires noting the sequential order of social events and specifying their formal qualities as well as their quantity.

The specification of sequential structures is an essential part of all scientific explanations. Astronomers specify the sequential order of celestial events; chemists those of inorganic phenomena; biologists of organic phenomena. In a similar fashion social scientists detect the sequential order of social phenomena. The most primitive form of sequential analysis is noting that when B occurs it is preceded by A. It is necessary to make across time observations of social phenomena in order to specify sequential orders; they cannot be specified by "point in time" observations of sets of objects (Saxton and Couch, 256: 1975).

One of the powers of video recordings is that the data they display allow for an across time mode of analysis; analysts of recordings are not limited to a point in time mode of analysis. The systematic study of recordings allows social scientists to specify how units of social action and social relationships evolve and devolve.

The specification of the formal properties of phenomena, the geometric dimensions, also is a critical facet of all scientific analyses. The beginning of scientific thought among Western Europeans was coterminus with the arise of geometry. The Copernican formulation of planetary movement offered a new specification of the relative position of the Sun, Moon, stars, and planets; it located the Sun, instead of the Earth, as the center of planetary movement. Copernicus' reformulation was a novel geometric ordering of celestial phenomena. He rearranged the locations of the heavenly bodies and thereby assigned them new formal properties. The emergence of modern chemistry rested on the specification of formal relations between chemical elements. Darwin and Mendel offered specifications of how new forms (species) emerged and how continuity of form was maintained across generations (Eiseley, 1961; Couch 1982). More recently the work of Watson and Crick (Judson, 1981) specified the geometric structure of DNA—the double helix.

Geometry is a powerful intellectual tool; it is a set of useful fictions. It asserts that there are perfect and universal forms. No two relationships are identical. Yet when phenomena are approached with a geometric frame of thought connections between elements and similarities of linkages between items can be observed. However, if social scientists are to develop formal theories of social phenomena they cannot slavishly adopt the geometry of the physical sciences, they will have to develop a social geometry. Simmel (1950) pioneered formal sociology; he called for the specification of the interconnectedness between interactants—the detection of elements of sociation.

Many sociologists have made numeric analyses of phenomena. Some of these analyses have been based upon highly intricate and very complex manipulations of algebraic formulae. However, these analyses have done little to advance our understanding of social phenomena. The emphasis on statistical analysis of quantities has been both misguided and premature.

Very few social scientists who emphasize quantification have given much attention to social process, social acts or social relationships. Instead most of them quantify the attributes of individuals or the products of human action. Some critics of quantitative analysis regard the quantification of social phenomena as an impossibility. In any event it will not be until after we have greater sophistication in specifying sequential orders and the formal properties of social phenomena that complex quantification procedures will be of much utility to social scientists interested in formulating principles of social processes. The quantification of the attributes or acts of individuals does not constitute a sociological analysis. It is a form of aggregate psychology.

SEQUENTIAL ORDER

The analyst of video recordings is confronted by an ever moving gestalt of social events of considerable complexity. Some facets of the data are constant; the clothing and physical appearance of the participants remain the same. These dimensions need to be noted, they are part of the context. But, the primary concern of analysts of social processes is events, not objects. To complete a sociolgical analysis it is necessary to note two different types of sequences. For some analyses it is necessary to note the sequences of initiating and responding acts of the individuals as they align their actions to produce units of social action. For other purposes it is necessary to note the sequential order of the production of elements of sociation. The first type of sequential order is specified by noting the acts of each interactant and how the acts of the two of them precede and follow one another. The second type of sequential order is specified by noting the joint acts of at least two individuals.

The specification of the sequential order of the acts of individuals is a necessary part of analyses when the objective is to characterize the type of relatedness the interactants establish and maintain. The objective of such analyses is not to specify the order of acts produced by an individual, rather it is to note which interactant intiated and which responded and how they fit together their acts. For example, one might note which interactant introduced a shared focus and which one acknowledged and accepted the shared focus. Analyses of this type provide a partial characterization of the form of relatedness interactants establish and maintain.

The careful examination of how interactants sequence their acts, who initiates and who responds, will often reveal critical dimensions of social relationships that are so taken for granted by both interactants and observers that their significance is often overlooked. For example, in the typical encounter of a representative and a dean in our studies of intergroup negotiation, the two of them greeted each other verbally, usually nodded in each other's direction, and usually the dean made a hand motion for the representative to take a seat which sometimes was accompanied by the statement "have a seat." In nearly all cases the representative simultaneously or with only a very brief delay produced a reciprocating and congruent line of activity. The two of them thereby activated an asymmetrical relationship. The dean was in charge.

In an exceptional case the representative was completely unresponsive to the dean's initiations and strode to the front of his desk and demanded, "How much time do I have?" The dean responded by offering his hand for a hand shake and stating, "As much as necessary." The representative grabbed the dean's hand and instituted a "radical hand shake" and asserted, "Don't give me any b—s—, how much time do I have?"

In this instance the taken for granted reciprocating sequences of acts that "normally" situated the participants in an asymmetrical relationship were not produced. The representative ignored the initiations of the dean, assumed the initiative and "forced" the dean to respond to her initiations. The typical initiation-response sequence was reversed. One consequence was these two negotiators activated quite a different social relationship than most others as they became situated as negotiators. The specification of sequences of reciprocating acts that activate a social relationship and situate people often provides insight into how social relationships frame social encounters and structure social endeavors. When out of the ordinary reciprocating sequences are compared with routine sequences that activate relationships the analysis may be especially revealing.

The replay and stop action features of video recordings provide researchers with the means to precisely specify the sequential order of reciprocating acts. These features of the technology can be abused. It is possible for analysts of video recordings to make far more refined specifications of sequences than can be made by the interactants themselves. For example, when a partisan group's representative enters the office of the dean one can determine with a high degree of interobserver reliability whether the dean pointed to the chair for the incomer before the incomer moved toward the chair even when it originally appears they acted simultaneously. However, a refined specification of a reciprocating sequence that is dependent upon the replay and stop action features of the technology can result in an analysis of questionable validity. If the observer of the recording makes the distinction, but it is a distinction that is impossible for the participants to make, it is a distinction of questionable validity. The precise specification of sequences of reciprocating acts that are dependent upon the technology can result in misleading characterizations of social encounters.

In the study of openings that isolated the elements of sociation that constitute elementary cooperative action three dyads moved from acting independently to acting in concert by both responding in unison. The members of these dyads "simultaneously evidenced a startled or freezing response, turned to each other and established eye contact, rose from their chairs and simultaneously moved toward the door together" (Miller, Hintz, and Couch, 1975: 12–13). The technology allowed for the specification of which member of each dyad moved first. However, both members of each of these three dyads claimed to have moved in unison in postsituation interviews; and, they appeared to move in unison when the recordings were played at normal speed. To specify reciprocating sequences in these cases would be to make an unauthentic characterization of their actions. The more valid characterization is that they moved simultaneously.

The specification of the temporal order of the production of elements of sociation is a second level of sequential analysis. Elements of sociation are produced by reciprocating acts that are noted by the interactants. For example, the establishment of a shared focus is a joint production. An indvidual can initiate a shared focus, but a shared focus is not established until another person responds to the intiation of the first person. The sequential orders of elements of sociation are specified by noting the sets of reciprocating acts that create each element of sociation. Some elements of sociation are produced by a sequence of individual acts as when one person calls for attention and another responds. Other elements of sociation are created by interactants simultaneously acting toward and responding to each other as when two people make eye contact upon hearing a loud sound. Some elements of sociation must be established before others. Reciprocal attention must be established before or simultaneous with social responsiveness.

The specification of the sequential order of elements of sociation is compounded by the fact that interactants, especially those with a robust shared past, can establish two or more elements of sociation at the same time. For example, when two long time employees establish eye contact and knowingly smile in unison the instant after their boss has made a mistake they instanteously establish several elements of sociation. They establish reciprocal attention, social responsiveness, an element of solidary responsiveness, and make a consensual negative assessment of their boss's competence.

The sequential order of the elements of sociation that compose a functional opening has been specified (Miller, Hintz, and Couch, 1975). The specification of the sequential order of the formation of complex forms of social action and social relationships is in its primitive stages. The sequential order of the elements of sociation that constitutes interpersonal negotiations (Sink and Couch, 1986) and those that make up social closings have been tentatively specified (Leichty, 1986). Sehested (1975) offers an outline of the sequential order for the establishment of solidary relationships. In a similar manner, Miller (1986a) offers a preliminary specification of the sequential order of the elements of sociation that result in the activation of a hypnotic encounter. However, for the most part the specification of the sequential order of elements of sociation that constitute various forms of social action and social relationships remains uncharted territory.

GEOMETRIC PATTERNS

Much of theoretical sociology implies a geometric mode of analysis. Sociologists employ the concepts social relationships, social structure, and social forms to refer to the character of relatedness between people. The observation and characterization of relatedness, relationships and structures requires concepts that denote how two or more elements are linked together.

Some of the linkages between human beings are relatively stable, but others are fleeting.

The stark geometry conveyed by points and lines is not adequate for the specification of the formal properties of social processes and social relationships. Many human relationships contain complexly intertwined elements of sociation; and the social connections between interactants are dynamic and pulsating. Some elements of sociation are relatively constant but other elements of sociation are more or less constantly modified as people align their actions to produce courses of social action. One moment one is in charge, but the next moment that same person may become a passive responder.

Human beings are capable of establishing and sustaining an almost indefinite variety of social linkages. They range in complexity and duration from that of two persons who fleetingly note each other's presence at a sporting event to the simultaneously affiliative and antagonistic elements of sociation that are present between a married couple who are deeply in love but have a long and convoluted history of confronting each other in the political arena. The geometric depiction of the latter relationship would require a far more complex geometric form than the double helix.

When compared to the complex relationships of married couples the relationships between strangers participating in a laboratory study are quite simple. Yet, even these encounters contain several social linkages. At the minimum, both acknowledge each other as a participant in a study, they mutually categorize each other on the basis of gender and age, they jointly locate themselves as subordinate to the researcher, they accept the identities assigned, and they attend to shared foci and act to achieve assigned objectives. Once they begin interacting they introduce additional elements of sociation.

Many of these linkages can be ignored. If the study is appropriately designed and run most of the linkages between the participants will be constant across sessions. Of course, the constancy is always a manner of degree. But, if participants have been effectively positioned then during the analysis attention can be focused on the differences in the forms of social relationships established in the two different contexts while presuming that the overarching context of a laboratory study has created a set of elements of sociation that are the same for all groups.

To detect the forms of relatedness created in the comparison groups it is necessary to conceptualize the acts of the interactants as a series of two points. However, the points are not static points, but dynamic entities. As interactants align their actions at least minor modifications in the linkages between the two of them will be made. The task of the analyst is to depict the everchanging quality of these linkages and how the changes made are associated with the social contexts that frame their encounters.

The geometric analysis of human action is further complicated by the fact that human beings can simultaneously sustain contradictory or discordant linkages. The prototype is love-hate relationships. Many married couples both love and dislike each other. On a less dramatic level, both bargaining and negotiating are forms of social action that contain discordant elements. Bargainers are usually simultaneously affiliative and antagonistic. Each is attracted to some service or object controlled by the other, recognizes his dependence on the other if he is to obtain the desired service or good, but at the same time each is usually interested in acquiring the greatest benefit at the least cost. The latter concern often generates antagonism between bargainers. In a similar manner negotiators mutually acknowledged they have a shared distal future but at the same time they mutually recognize that each wishes the future to be structured in a way that conflicts with the wishes of the other.

Geometric analyses of social processes attempt to specify the formal features of social encounters; the form of the action and/or social relationship. A third party point of view is adopted by the analyst. The analyst notes the actions of the interactants and characterizes their relatedness from his position. The standpoint of each of the interactants may be adopted during the analysis, but the depiction of their relatedness is not made from the standpoint of either of the interactants.

It is very easy for analysts to become intrigued with and adopt the standpoint of one of the interactants. That can yield insight into the phenomena under examination, but it can also lead a researcher to overlook significant phenomena. To complete an analysis from a third party perspective it is necessary for the analyst to note not just the standpoints and activities of one person or the other, but standpoints and the activities of both parties and the fit between the two.

The linkages established by strangers in a laboratory are impoverished when compared to the linkages established by interactants that have a vibrant shared past. Nonetheless, the specification of the linkages between members of dyads and triads of strangers and between them and their environment within a laboratory is a very complex endeavor, it is so complex that it is impossible to detect and characterize all of them. The complexity is increased by the fact that the linkages are not constant. Therefore, the specification of elements of sociation that prevail within a group is never complete. Rather, the analyst focuses his attention on only activities that are deemed significant for formulating an explanation of some of the features of the social processes or social relationships under analysis.

By adopting a geometric frame of thought and focusing on the reciprocating of acts that establish elements of sociation it is possible to detect both short lived and enduring relations within acting units. To accomplish this it is necessary for the analyst to focus on reciprocating acts that form and transform the connections between the participants. The relations at a point in time are noted, but it is also necessary to recognize that as interaction continues the relatedness changes.

QUANTIFICATION

It is relatively easy to quantify the acts of individuals when video recordings are analyzed. The number of head nods by each person or the number of "O.K.s" offered by each can be accurately counted and a high level of interobserver reliability can be achieved. The ease of quantification can be a trap. The objective of a sociological analysis is to specify how they, a plurality of persons, produce coordinated action and social relationships. The number of times a person says "O.K." within an encounter is far less important than how a given "O.K." fits in with the preceding and following actions of the other person. Each act acquires its significance by how it fits with the preceding, simultaneous, and following acts of another person.

In our study of the representative relationship in which half of the triads had an independent source of information about what had transpired during the intergroup negotiations and the other half did not, a cursory examination of the transcripts indicated that the constituents in the "no news" groups spoke less frequently and made shorter statements than did the constituents of the "news" groups. We did not, although it could have easily been done, count either the number of words or utterances offered by the constituents in the two different contexts. Had we counted the number of statements offered by constituents and made a statistical test of the differences it would have been highly significant. To have ended the analysis at that point would have been an example of misplaced concreteness; and, an example of an aborted analysis.

After noting the disparity between the two sets of groups we then proceeded to note if the statements offered by the constituents were acknowledged, accepted, elaborated or modified by other members of their group. The concept "having a say" emerged to characterize one element of sociation established in some of the groups. We refined the concept by specifying that "having a say" occurred when a constituent made a statement that characterized the intergroup negotiations that was accepted, modified, or elaborated by another member of the group. If one person made a statement, but that statement was not attended to in any way, and was simply ignored, the act was treated as a "nonevent". An individual produced an act but the act did not become part of the consensual definition of the intergroup negotiations that was established within the group.

Once the criteria have been established for a given element of sociation or form of social action, then the ratio of the presence of these social items within the two different contexts can be noted. The number or percentages of groups that achieved an objective within a specific context can be noted and compared with the number or percentage of groups that completed the objective within a different context. For example, it was noted that is 18 of the 19 groups with an independent source of information about the intergroup negotiations the constituents had a say in characterizing the nature of the intergroup negotiations; whereas in only 5 of the 15 "no news" groups did the constituents have a say (Katovich, Weiland, and Couch,

1981). That difference informs us that partisan groups with an independent source of information are more likely to participate in meaningful discussion of the situation than those who do not have an independent source of information.

CONCLUSIONS

To formulate principles of social processes and relationships it is necessary to make the activities of a dyad the minimum unit of analysis. Sociological principles cannot be formulated by noting the frequency of types of acts produced by individuals. Rather, analysts must proceed by noting the sequences of acts produced by persons as they join their individual lines of action together to construct courses of social action. Sometimes, elements of sociation are produced by sequenced reciprocal acts; other times, as when people make eye contact, elements of sociation are produced as persons simultaneously respond to and act toward each other.

Different elements of sociation are combined in various ways to produce forms of social action and forms of social relationships. In some instances the elements of sociation that constitute forms of social action and relationships are produced in a fixed sequence. For example, before interactants can be socially responsive they must first be reciprocally attentive. One of the tasks of sociologists is to specify the necessary sequential order, if there is one, that results in the establishment of a form of social action or social relationship.

The detection and delineation of the elements of sociation and social forms requires the analyst to adopt a geometric standpoint toward the phenomena. Elements of sociation are linkages between interactants and linkages between them and their environment; social relationships are composed of complexly intertwined elements of sociation.

The sequential and formal order of social life is a constructed order. It is produced by people as they act with, toward, and for each other. Social orders are human creations. To create them, human beings must give attention to each other and respond to each other. These activities are readily observeable—they can be seen and heard. The difficulties of developing general propositions about social life do not stem from the unobservability of the phenomena, but from the complexity of the phenomena and a failure to apply the proper frame of thought to the phenomena. Social life is not static; it has only a relative constancy in the best of conditions. Evolution, devolution, modifications, and transformations continually occur. Constancy of relationships is achieved only when persons actively attempt to maintain a given form of relatedness.

Through the detection of repetitive sequences of reciprocating acts, the sequential order of the production of various elements of sociation and the delineation of forms of relatedness we will achieve greater understanding of social life. That objective cannot be achieved by quantifying the activities and attributes of individuals. The quantification of the acts of individuals often can be an important first step in the analysis of social phenomena. But, to complete an analysis of social processes quantification must be subordinated to and integrated with sequential and geometric analyses.

Chapter XI

Formulating Abstract Propositions

The objective of formulating universal principles of social life has informed the efforts of sociologists from the foundation of the discipline. Conte, who is generally regarded as the grandfather of sociology, called for the formation of "social physics." Durkheim, who is generally regarded as the father of sociology, reiterated the call for a search for laws of social phenomena. Both Comte and Durkheim presumed that the mechanical paradigm of classical physics provided a frame of thought that could, with minor modifications, be applied to social phenomena. However, that frame of thought has proven to be inadequate for the analysis of social phenomena (Couch, 1982).

Simmel (1950) and Mead (1934) offer an alternative approach to social phenomena for formulating generic propositions. Simmel advocated that social phenomena be approached in the same way that a grammarian approaches languages. He stated that if sociologists approached social phenomena by focusing attention not on the content, but on the formal properties of the content it would be possible to formulate general laws of human conduct. Mead formulated a position that stemmed from the Darwinian tradition. The Darwinian paradigm, in contrast to the paradigm derived from Newtonian physics, postulates that variation (change) is as viable a dimension of the world as is constancy. One of the guiding dictums of the evolutionary paradigm is a call for the analysis of both constancy and change.

Both Simmel and Mead held that if a science of social life

was to be constructed it would be necessary to detect and articulate the structure of social processes and relationships. The central questions that flow from that position are: What are the basic elements of social processes, how are those elements combined to produce various types of social processes and relationships, what consequences flow from the different types of processes and relationships, and how is constancy (order) achieved. The mechanical paradigm conceptualizes phenomena as objects that maintain a steady state; in contrast, the frame of thought called for by Mead and Simmel recognizes that both constancy and change are simultaneously viable facets of social phenomena.

Analytic induction has been offered as a methological procedure that is consistent with the epistemology of Simmel Mead (Turner, 1953). Analytic induction calls for the systematic analysis of sets of data to formulate general laws of human conduct. Most sociologists who have advocated analytic induction have generated data through naturalistic observation. They have been almost as unsuccessful in the formulation of generic principles of social life as have those who have generated data by administering questionnaires and made statistical analyses of questionnaire responses. Their relative lack of success in formulating universal principles of social phenomena stems, in part, from the fact that many who have used the principles of analytic induction have not used comparison groups (Cressy, 1953; Emerson, 1970; Farberman, 1975). Other field researchers have acquired data from two or more research sites and applied the principles of analytic induction to their data (Glaser and Strauss, 1967; Hall and Spencer-Hall, 1982) with the objective of formulating generic principles.

However, when data are generated by making naturalistic observations of social processes in the field the rapidity and complexity of social phenomena make it almost impossible for unaided naturalistic observers to acquire data that are complete and precise enough to allow for the formulation of viable generic propositions about social phenomena. Perhaps generic principles can be formulated on the basis of unaided field observations if the observations are clearly focused and if the research sites are selected with care (O'Toole and Dubin, 1968; Hall and Neitz, 1986).

The laboratory in conjunction with video recordings provide researchers with processual data that is sufficiently complete and precise to formulate abstract generic propositions about social phenomena. However, while recordings provide processual data of high fidelity, the data do not automatically result in the formulation of generic principles. Generic propositions of social life can only be formulated if the data are approached with that objective in mind.

The formulation of viable abstract propositions of social phenomena requires a dynamic interplay between theory and data. Theories provide analysts with abstract frames of thought that inform the examination of the data; the data are approached with the intention of constructing a theory or modifying and elaborating a theory. The development of generic principles of social phenomena requires the analyst to continually play the data and the informing theory against each other. Theories structure the examination of data; and the analysis of data in turn acts back upon the theory. The purpose is not to test and either verify or disprove a theory, but to build a theory that rests upon a sound empirical foundation, or, to modify and extend an established theory on the basis of data. When theory and data are played off against each other, priority is given to the data. No theory is sacrosanct.

Unless data are interfaced with a theoretical framework they will not contribute to the formulation of valid abstract assertions. The accumulation of data may provides facts, but unless the data are seated within a theoretical framework they will not contribute to an understanding of phenomena. Nearly all events noted by social scientists, including those observed by laboratory researchers who record social encounters, have been noted before by many others. Social closings have been observed millions of times, but a formal theory of social closings was not advanced until Leichty (1986) examined recordings of sets of them with the intent of offering a formal theory of social closings. In one sense social scientists do not generate any new data. Rather, they focus upon carefully selected "facts" with the intention of using those facts to formulate general principles.

Theoretical considerations inform the efforts of most laboratory researchers long before data are acquired. Although some research undertakings are informed only by a concern with generating data that bear upon some practical problem. In either event it is during the analysis of the laboratory generated data that theoretical considerations come to the fore. The overarching objective of theoretically driven analyses is to formulate monothetic statements about phenomena, and to articulate statements that characterize a given set of phenomena in a manner that is universally true. In their ideal form universal statements assert that each and every time a given condition prevails certain specific combinations of events have occurred.

Glaser and Strauss (1967) issued a call for the construction of formal theories of social processes through induction—by giving priority to data. They call their approach grounded theory. They call for first formulating a substantive theory; namely, an abstract characterization of observations that are acquired by the thorough study of a particular social context. Movement toward a formal theory is achieved by constantly comparing two or more substantive theories with each other. For example, one might first construct a theory of nurse-patient interaction based upon observations of nurse-patient interaction and a theory of physican-nurse interaction based upon observations of physician-nurse interaction. Glaser and Strauss call these characterizations substantive theories. Those interested in the formulation of a formal theory of asymmetric interactions might then compare and contrast the theories of interaction patterns derived from the two different research sites to construct a formal theory of asymmetric interaction.

Much the same procedure is followed when video recordings of specimens are analyzed. However, one of the differences is that if the research is properly designed, video recordings of specimens of interaction in two similar, but somewhat different, contexts will be available for examination. The patterns of interaction from the two different contexts can then be compared and contrasted with the objective of formulating an abstract set of statements that accurately and comprehensively characterize the phenomena for all cases.

Naturalistic observers who advocate analytic induction presume that unaided observations of naturally occurring phenomena will generate data that are sufficiently focused and uncluttered to allow for the formulation accurate and invariant propositions. Naturalistic observation, at least as practiced by

Glaser and Strauss (1964), has advanced our understanding of some basic social phenomena. However, the major thrust of grounded theorizing based on unaided observations of social phenomena has been the specification of the nature of relatedness between persons. Relatively little attention has been given by naturalistic observers to the specification of the sequential ordering of elements of sociation that compose various forms of social relatedness. The lack of attention to sequential order by naturalistic observers stems in part from the limitations of the data acquired via naturalistic observations. Such observations seldom are complete and accurate enough to allow for the precise specification of the sequential order of the construction of the elements of sociation that constitute various forms of social action and social relationships.

Glaser and Strauss, and most other advocates of analytic induction for the construction of formal theories of social phenomena, advocate a processual ontology (Hall and Neitz, 1986). They also recognize the necessity of systematic, selective, and sustained confrontation of social pheonmena, but they fail to recognize the necessity of a theory driven analysis and the necessity of an intense interface between theory and data.

It is very difficult to acquire data that retains the processual features of social activity unless one's observations are enhanced with recording devices. Human memory, aided only by field notes, usually is simply too inexact to provide the data necessary for the formulation of invarient abstract propositions about social phenomena that includes the specification of the sequential order of the production of elements of sociation.

Recordings provide processual data of social phenomena that are far more complete and accurate than are the data obtained by naturalistic observations. The data provided by recordings allow for the specification of the sequential order of elements of sociation as well as the specification of how people establish and maintain forms of relatedness.

The specifications of universal laws requires two types of constant comparison. On the one hand, it is necessary to, at the minimum, constantly compare the observations made in one context with those made in a similar but slightly different context. On the other hand, it is also necessary to constantly compare the order specified or implied by the theory that informs the analysis with the sequential order displayed by the data. The first type of comparison, for example, can be achieved by comparing the evolution and transformation of the representative relationship when a closed awareness context prevails between the representative and her constitutes with the evolution and transformation of the representative relationship when an open awareness context prevails between the representative and her constitutes (Weiland and Couch, 1986). The second type of comparison is made by comparing current theoretical statements about the nature of the representative relationship with the patterns of behavior and the sequential order of their production that is displayed in the recordings of transactions between representatives and their constituents.

Those researchers who attempt to formulate abstract assertions about social processes confront the data with the intention of constantly comparing and contrasting data acquired from two different contexts and constantly interfacing theory and data. To achieve the objective of formulating abstract valid assertions it is often necessary to (1) reframe the question, (2) reconceptualize the phenomena, or (3) note phenomena previously ignored. Often two or more of the above steps must be taken before it is possible to formulate a universal abstract assertion. The adequate analysis of data requires that the analyst be flexible but disciplined.

REFRAMING THE QUESTION

It is a mundane, but true, observation that many times a key to achieving greater comprehension of phenomena is asking the right question. The sociological enterprise in general has been stymied in part due to the fact that many sociologists have insisted upon asking the wrong question. The critical question for many has been: How can we predict the behavior of human beings? Except in the most gross terms, that is impossible except under controlled conditions. The prediction of human activity under uncontrolled conditions is similar to predicting the weather on the basis of one's aching bones; or, predicting what new species will evolve in the next ten-thousand years. One can make such predictions; the predictions of laymen are almost as good as those of the experts. The more viable questions are:

How are given forms of social action and social relationships constructed; and, given a specific form of social relatedness under a particular condition what are the consequences that are likely to follow? The task of analysts is to specify the elements of sociation that a plurality of people must produce to create a given form of social action or social relationships and what are the likely consequences of a given social relationship within a given context? (Hardesty, 1986a). If the analysis dedicated to the specification of the elements and structure of a given form of social action or a given social relationship is successful then it is possible to specify that each and every time a given form of social action is produced a distinctive set of elements of sociation was created and the sequential order of their production. If the analysis is directed toward providing information about the consequences of forms of social action or social relationships then if it is successful, it will be possible to state that when X form of relatedness is created within Y context it is likely that one of the consequences will be A.

Researchers nearly always have some ideas on what are the elements of sociation that compose a given form of social action or social relationships before they begin their analysis of the data. The data are then examined to note the presence or absence of the elements and their sequential order of production. However, on many occasions it is impossible to answer the question that originally frames the analysis. On other occasions, it is possible to answer the original question, but when the answer is achieved the researcher recognizes that the answer is trivial.

When we began the analysis of the data set used to specify the elements and structure of social openings the analysis was informed by the question: What reciprocating sets of acts must people produce to move from a state of copresence to the production of coordinated action? That formulation of the question was partially derived from the earlier work of Schegloff (1968) on openings. He offered the ABABAB sequence to characterize social openings. Namely that A acted followed by B acting, followed in turn by A acting, etc. However, as we began to analyze the data it became apparent that the ABABAB format was not adequate. The interactants often noted each other's actions and acted toward the other at the same time. In many instances their actions could not be fitted into the ABAB format.

For example, some of those dyads established reciprocal acknowledged attention, not by A acting toward B and B in turn acting toward A, but by the interactants making eye contact and simultaneously smiling at each other. That observation enticed us to reformulate the question to: What elements of sociation must a dyad establish to move from a condition of acting independently in each other's presence to acting interdependently?

The reframing of the question led us to simultaneously attend to the acts of both parties instead of first the acts of person A and then the acts of person B. We were then able to specify that the construction of all social openings required the establishment of reciprocal attention, social responsiveness, congruent functional identities, a shared focus and a social objective. Furthermore, we were able to specify that reciprocal attention was always established prior to the production of social responsiveness and that social responsiveness was always established prior to the establishment of congruent functional identities. A shared focus may be established at the same moment as reciprocal attention is established or it may not be produced until congruent functional identities are established. But in all cases a shared focus is established before a social objective. Both the elements and their necessary sequential order were specified. "The elements and structure are neither cultural, location, nor population bound" (Couch, 1984: 7).

In this instance it was impossible to answer the original question posed. The question that we first applied to the data did not allow us to recognize that human beings can attend and act simultaneously. As the analysis proceeded, we recognized that if a comprehensive and adequate characterization of how people constructed social openings was to be offered it would be necessary to provide a formulation that incorporated simultaneous reciprocating acts into our answer. To acquire an adequate answer it was necessary to reframe the question. However, even when the question was reframed it did not allow us to formulate a generic proposition that characterized all of the cases under examination. Three deviant cases remained. The formulation of a universal abstract assertion that included these three deviant cases required that we reconceptualize the data under examination.

RECONCEPTUALIZATION

All human experiences are partially structured by the standpoint of the observer. That is as true of the experiences of researchers when analyzing data as it is of all others. Two rabid sports fans cheering for opposing teams, even if seated next to each other, literally see different events; and, they are even more likely to make different interpretations of the events that both note. Facts do not exist independent of an observer; and the facts for each observer are a partial reflection of the standpoint of each observer.

Theoretical perspectives provide standpoints. They imply that certain pheonmena are important and that other phenomena are insignificant. The sociological tradition provides the general standpoint that it is necessary to attend to social phenomena if one is to formulate general principles of social processes. In addition, most researchers have rather specific concepts that direct their attention to certain phenomena which at the same time often leads them to overlook or ignore other phenomena. Furthermore, the concepts implicitly direct researchers to see and hear the phenomena under examination in a specific manner. Sometimes, the concepts only vaguely orient the researcher; other times they rather precisely orient the researcher. In either event it is often necessary to modify concepts, discard concepts and to formulate new concepts before it is possible to formulate adequate abstract propositions. When there is a clash between established conceptual formulations and the date, primacy is always given to the data. The data are obdurate; theories are tentative.

Nearly every researcher recognizes that the theory that informs an analysis directs attention to certain aspects and away from other aspects of the data; and, that it is sometimes necessary to free oneself of the limitations imposed by the theory to complete an analysis. However, it is less generally recognized that how researchers approach their data is also influenced by nontheoretical taken for granted ideas. For example, when researchers design a study to examine a specific type of social action there is a tendency to presume that each episode designed to elicit a given form of social action does in fact elicit that form of social action. However, in some instances the participants do not produce the specimens of social action anticipated. The social context that participants activate within the laboratory is sometimes not the one the researchers presume they will activate.

When we designed the studies of intergroup negotiations we presumed that when the two representatives met in the intergroup negotiation episodes that they would in fact engage in intergroup negotiations. And in nearly all cases they did. However, in a few instances when the two representatives met in the intergroup negotiation episode they did not negotiate. We orginally attempted to analyze those transactions by treating the encounter as if the two representatives were negotiating. It was not until someone not intimately involved in the research effort who was viewing a troublesome recording with us asserted, "I don't know what those two are doing, but they are not negotiating." Only then did we "step back" and ask ourselves the question, "Do all of the episodes that we programmed to elicit intergroup negotiations display instances of intergroup negotiations?" In this particular case the two "representatives" met in the intergroup negotiation room. But, they did not activate their categorical identities of representatives nor did they establish mutually recognized collective differences as their shared focus. Instead, they engaged in a convoluted discussion and debate that centered on their personal differences regarding the proper place of women in modern society.

The formulation of the propositions that adequately characterized social openings required major theoretical reconceptualizations. One of the major reconceptualizations was to regard the acts of the dyad, not the sequential reciprocating acts of individuals as the unit of analysis. To achieve that level of analysis it was necessary to replace concepts such as initiating act and acknowledged act with the concept "reciprocally acknowledged attention." The former concepts directed our attention to the activities of the individuals who composed the dyads. In contrast, the latter concept directed our attention to activities produced by the dyad. It was only after the activities of the dyad were explicitly conceptualized as the focus of concern that we were able to adequately characterize the data displayed by the video recordings.

In a similar manner, it was necessary to elaborate upon an

original conceptualization that directed our attention to the display of intentions by each member of the dyad. That conceptualization was modify to included a concern with whether or not the intentions displayed by one individual were noted by the other member of the dyad.

These reconceptualizations allowed us to formulate a general principle that adequately characterized the activities of 43 of the 46 dyads. However, three deviant cases remained that violated our general principle. These three dyads did not produce the elements of sociation in the sequential order. The members of these three dyads immediately began acting in concert the moment a shared focus was established. The examination and re-examining of the recordings did not allow us to satisfactorily characterize their actions. They did not first establish reciprocal attention, then social responsiveness and then project congruent functional identities. They did not go through the sequence of establishing first one element of sociation and then the next.

These three deviant cases were the source of considerable consternation. It was not until we directed attention to additional data not contained in the recordings that we were able to formulate a resolution. Two additional sources of data and a major reconceptualization of the problem finally allow us to formulate a set of integrated statements that characterized all social openings. One additional source of data was the questionnaires that all participants had completed. Those data informed us that the members of all three deviant dyads were long standing friends. They had attended high school together and were sharing a room at the time the study was completed. The other additional source of data was from a study of social openings on telephones (Hintz, 1974). One of the observations derived from the telephonic openings was that telephonic openings constructed by strangers took an entirely different form than those constructed by acquaintances. When acquaintances contacted each other by telephone they nearly always produced reciprocating acts that acknowledged their shared past and then introduced a shared focus and social objective. The acknowledgement of their shared past typically was nothing more than a reciprocating "hi" "hi".

Those observations indicated that when people have a shared past they can and often do construct openings in a different way than do strangers. They can use their shared past to quickly situate themselves with each other. It is not necessary for aquaintances to sequentially produce each element of sociation in order to coordinate their actions. Voice recognition and their shared past allows them to produce all of the elements of sociation in an instant. Those with a shared past can produce all of the elements of sociation necessary for cooperative behavior vertically instead of sequentially.

These observations led us to conclude that in the three deviant cases when the members of these dyads made eye contact following the noise eminating from the other room, they were able to act in unison by each making the assumption the other would respond in the same manner. "The assumption of mutual responsiveness and congruent functional identities were validated by each simultaneously noting that self and other were in fact taking a parallel line of action" (Miller, Hintz, and Couch, 1975: 13). In contrast, strangers have no firm basis upon which to assume how the other will respond. Consequently when they construct a social opening they usually produce the elements of sociation in a sequential order.

The reconceptualizations that allowed for the formulation of a universal statement on how people move from acting independently to act interdependently also made us aware that human action not only occurs across time; but that, in addition, social action is temporally structured. Namely, that human beings use their past in the present to structure their actions.

Those specimens of interaction that originally appear to be deviant cases often provide the stimulus for the formulation of a more inclusive theory. However, in many cases it is necessary to formulate major reconceptualizations in order to develop a comprehensive theory. To formulate a more inclusive theory it is usually necessary to constantly compare and contrast the "deviant" cases with the "normal" ones. If attention is limited to only the deviant cases or only to the normal ones it is unlikely that the necessary reconceptualizations will be made.

NOTING OVERLOOKED PHENOMENA

Phenomena that are "right before one's eyes" and critical to the formulation of a more adequate explanation are frequently overlooked. Long before Darwin formulated the theory of evolution many biologists had noted across generation variation. But, none assigned any significance to the variation. Darwin, in contrast, assigned significance to across generation variation. In addition, he interfaced those observations with the observations that each generation produced a larger population than itself; but that only a percentage of each generation matured and in turn produced a subsequent generation. Whereas other biologists who had noted variation across generation dismissed the observation as of no consequence, Darwin concluded that the variation across generation in conjunction with failure of all young to survive and reproduce was of consequence. He was thereby able to formulate the theory of evolution.

It simply is not possible to note of all events. That is especially the case when the objects of analysis are specimens of social action. The theoretical frame of thought that researchers bring to bear to the data also often leads them to overlook critical phenomena.

When we began our studies of the representative relationship the concept "nonresponsiveness" was not a part of our conceptual framework. In one study based on triads composed of friends (Katovich, Weiland and Couch, 1981) we noted that some of the representatives lost control of their behavior during the accounting sessions when they were reporting the outcome of the intergroup negotiation sessions to their two constituents. They often stuttered, moved in a jerky manner, and repeated themselves. We were at a loss to explain that rather distinctive activity. We had not noted that type of behavior in other studies where the partisan groups were populated with strangers, nor did all of the representatives of the partisan groups composed of friends produce these rather distinctive behaviors.

Again, it was an observation of someone not involved with the study that first alerted us to the phenomenon that allowed us to formulate an explanation of the loss of control on the part of the representative. She noted, "Look at those two constituents, they're like lumps on a log. Are those guys friends?" We then directed our attention to nonactivity as well as activity. We then quickly recognized that the nonresponsiveness of the constituents was apparent to the representative and a source of consternation for him. When people are situated and one of them is acting and the other does not act, makes no response, the failure to act is itself an act. Or, in a cliche, when people are copresent they cannot not act. Nonresponsiveness is a very powerful act, especially when it occurs in encounters between friends committed to a shared objective. Nonresponsiveness communicates to the other that all is not well; that one is unhappy with what the other is doing or has done.

In this case, and many others what was at first not regarded as a phenomenon was in fact a critical phenomenon. Activities that at first did not seem important were important for both the interactants and for researchers attempting to formulate an explanation of the encounters.

The reverse also is sometimes the case. Often when the analysis begins researchers make the presumption that certain specific phenomena are important for the development of a comprehensive explanation of the encounters, but as the analysis proceeds, it becomes apparent that the phenomena originally regarded as critical are insignificant.

CONCLUSIONS

The analysis of recorded specimens of social action is relatively uncharted territory. There are no well formulated guidelines. That is especially the case when the form of activity under examination has not previously been studied in the laboratory and the objective is to formulate viable abstract assertions about the phenomena under investigation. No formulae are available. The successful completion of such analyses requires the analyst to adopt a flexible standpoint toward the data, be willing to reframe the question, attempt reconceptualizations, and to be sensitive to facets of the data that may not at first seem significant.

If the objective is to formulate abstract and accurate assertions, that objective must continually be kept in the forefront as the data analysis proceeds. If that objective is not kept in the forefront it is very easy to become overwhelmed with the data. The data that analysts of recordings confront is far richer and more complex than the data that must be managed by a questionnaire researcher. Many, when they first undertake such analyses, conclude that the data are unmanageable. And, they are unmanageable unless the data are addressed with a question or a limited number of questions in hand that focus the attention of the analyst. But, if the data are approached in a disciplined but flexible manner it is possible to manage the data and to formulate abstract assertions about social processes that rest upon a far firmer base than those formulated on the bases of questionnaire responses or field notes.

However, an analysis is never completed by simply exposing oneself to the data. All analyses are framed by one or more theories, although in many cases the theory is only a vague set of ideas. Usually attention is focused on those social acts that contribute to or militate against the formation of a particular form of social process or social relationship (Hardesty, 1986a). The intent of the researcher is to detect and specify the structure of the social phenomena under consideration.

Sensitizing concepts (Blumer, 1969) and working hypothesis structure the early steps of the analysis. On occasion the working hypothesis is no more specific than "when x and y occur in sequence a very distinctive form of relatedness is established." Close attention is given to the data; anomalies are given special attention. The analysis is guided by the objectives of transforming sensitizing concepts into definitive concepts and working hypotheses into generic principles.

The analysis proceeds by comparing recorded specimens of social acts from two different contexts. The general procedure is similar to the constant comparative method of Glaser and Strauss (1967: 101–117), but differs in that the specimens compared are derived from theoretically specified contexts that were formulated when the study was designed and the fact that recordings and transcripts, not field notes and memories, provide the data.

Often the research act begins with a general and imprecise question. The question is given somewhat greater specificity when the study is designed. Once the data are generated attention is focused on concrete social phenomena. The level of abstraction, the degree of precision of the concepts, and of linkages between phenomena are usually low when the analysis begins. Through the examination of the data, the reformulation of the question and redefinition of concepts the analyst moves to higher levels of abstraction and precision. Sometimes to achieve the level of abstraction and/or precision desired it is necessary to retreat to an earlier stage of the research act and start over (Hardesty, 1986a) (see Diagram XI.1).

Generic principles derived from recordings have far greater validity than those derived from data that only indirectly reflect the processual quality of human life. If social scientists are to formulate generic principles—develop a science of social life—they will have to recognize that human life only exists in process, develop procedures for generating data that displays social processes with high fidelity, undertake disciplined analyses of the data, and base their generalizations on data that can be shared with others. If those dictums are accepted, it may be possible to develop theories of social processes and relationships that have a much firmer foundation than current theories do.

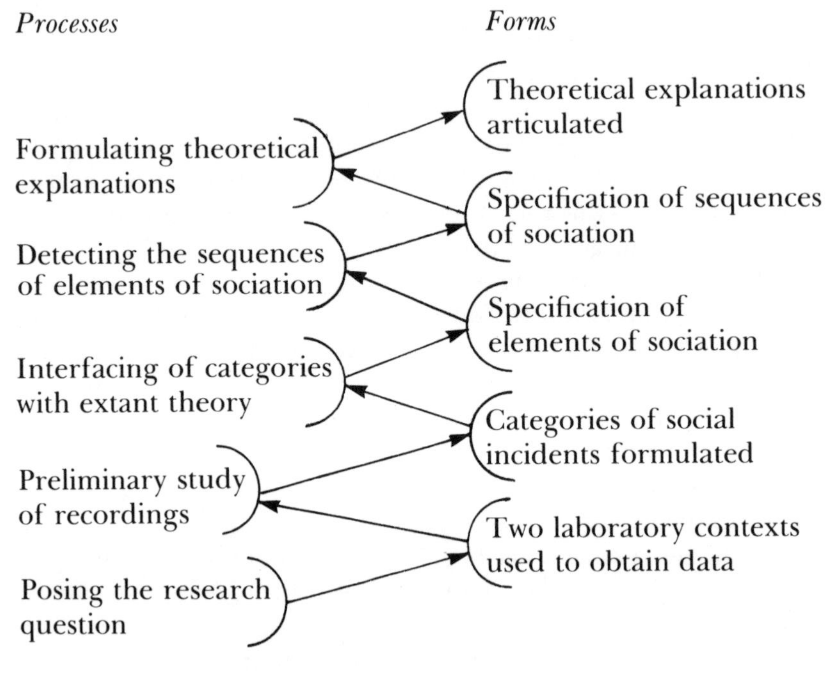

Notes:
To be read from the bottom up.
*Adopted from Hardesty (1986a).

Diagram XI. 1. Steps Toward the Formulation of Generic Principles*

Chapter XII

The Sociological Tradition and the Laboratory

The sociological tradition has contributed little to the laboratory research completed by sociologists and laboratory research has contributed little to sociology. The failure of laboratory research to contribute much to sociology stems from the failure of many sociologists who undertake laboratory studies to use the sociological tradition and their sociological imaginations. Many of them fail to design studies that elicit social phenomena and/or fail to maintain a sociological standpoint when analyzing their data. Most have failed to recognize the simple, but basic, facts that the completion of sociological research requires making activities of dyads the minimum unit of analysis and that human existence is processual. In addition, many have failed to properly conceptualize the nature of the social encounter between researchers and volunteers at the laboratory.

Other sociologists (Blumer, 1969, 1980) have concluded that the subject matter of sociologists, social processes, and relationships is not amendable to laboratory procedures. Many critics of laboratory research make the mistake of presuming laboratory research can only be completed by those who accept the tenets of positivism and apply the mechanical paradigm to human conduct. As Katovich (1985: 49) notes, these critics of laboratory research regard it "as an extension of a paradigmatic point of view that reifies variables as independent movers of men." Usually the critics also claim laboratory research is artificial and maintain that sociological research must be "directed to a given empirical world in its natural, ongoing character instead of a simulation of such a world or to an abstraction from it (as in the case of laboratory experimentation)" (Blumer, 1969:46).

These criticisms are well founded only when laboratory research of social phenomena is equated with a particular research tradition. Namely those laboratory studies beginning with the work of Bales (1950) on through to the current research contextualized by expectation states and exchange theory wherein the responses of individuals in various contexts, not the social activities of people, are made the units of analysis.

The use of the laboratory and recording devices does not require the adoption of a frame of thought that makes static attributes of individuals the units of analysis; nor does it require acceptance of the positivistic ontology. Social processes as well as the behavior of individuals can be studied in the laboratory. How people create social phenomena can be studied as well as how social phenomena structure the actions of individuals. If the dictates of positivism are used to structure the generation and analysis of data, it is a certainty that laboratory research of human conduct will contribute little to sociology.

AN IRONIC HISTORY

The history of laboratory research of social phenomena is doubly ironic. First, some of the earliest laboratory studies of human conduct were far more sociological than many of the recent ones. Second, the outstanding early studies of human conduct that were informed by a sociological frame of thought were completed by researchers trained as psychologists, not by sociologists. Some of these early studies addressed basic sociological issues. In general, as sociologists began conducting laboratory studies, the research became less sociological.

Over 50 years ago Sherif completed a series of laboratory studies that demonstrated how dyads construct social standards of perception and how these social standards once developed endure and structure the subsequent perceptions of individuals (Sherif, 1935, 1936). He thereby provided a sound empirical illustration of Durkheim's (1915) seminal insight that the products of social interaction structure the subsequent behavior of both groups and individuals.

About the same time Lewin and his associates completed a series of studies of how the structure of groups impacts upon the experiences and subsequent behavior of members of groups. Among other things, they demonstrated that authoritarian groups generated apathy and submissive behavior whereas democratic groups displayed more involvement and independence (Lewin, Lippett and White 1939). The accomplishments of Lewin and his associates, like that of Sherif, were contingent upon using the laboratory to convene groups and make detailed observations of their conduct. It is also worthy of note that Lewin did not deceive his participants. They were convened, provided with a social context, and asked to complete assigned tasks.

Several laboratory studies of social phenomena were completed shortly after World War II. Swanson (1953), for example, convened triads in the laboratory to examine dimensions of human conduct distinctive to crowds. His study demonstrated that contrary to the accepted sociological theorizing of the time that no special set of concepts is required to explain the actions of people in crowds; that so-called crowd behavior is but a variant of routine interaction. Rose and Felton (1955) convened small groups to examine how the invention, diffusion, adoption, and stability of cultural elements were related to changes in the membership of groups.

These two studies, others could be cited, were informed by the sociological tradition and the researchers used their sociological imaginations to design the studies. The participants in these studies were convened, assigned social objectives, and allowed (required) to interact. These researchers also maintained a sociological standpoint when they analyzed their data.

Despite several promising studies of social phenomena by sociologists during the decade following World War II, laboratory studies of social phenomena did not flourish. As sociologists made greater use of the laboratory the studies became less sociological. The failure of sociological laboratory studies to mature as they might have seems to have been the consequence of three interrelated developments.

One of these developments was that laboratory studies of human conduct became prominent in psychology. The foci of concern of psychologists are, of course, different from those of sociologists. The basic unit of analysis for psychologists is not the group, social processes or units of social action, but transactions between an individual and his environment. Psychological laboratory researchers developed refined procedures for measuring the responses of individuals; for the most part, they were not concerned with social action. Many sociologists who undertook laboratory studies adopted the procedures developed by psychologists. That, of course, resulted in them making observations of the responses of individuals to stimuli, not of social action.

A second development that delayed the maturation of laboratory studies of social phenomena was the publication of Bales' *Interaction Process Analysis.* The procedures specified by Bales (1950) called for convening small groups in the laboratory. The participants were called upon to interact with one another and units of social action were elicited. However, the analytic dictums of Bales focused attention not upon social processes or social products, but upon the acts of individuals. He noted, "the group as a whole is not recognized as an actor" (Bales, 1968: 466). His procedures gave no recognition of collective action or of collective accomplishments. Sociological concepts were conspicuously absent from his guidelines for the analysis of data. Instead, he called for the quantification of the activities of individuals in the presence of others.

The third development that inhibited the development of laboratory studies of social processes and relationships was the emergence of statistics as the primary mode of analysis by sociologists. Statistics, the analysis of statics, direct attention to objects, not to processes. Many who used the laboratory presumed that statistical analysis was an inherent part of all scientific analysis. Consequently, they attended only to phenomena that were amendable to statistical analysis. Statistical procedures call for a point in time, instead of an across time mode of analysis (Saxton and Couch, 1975). A sociological analysis of human conduct requires not only an across time examination of social phenomena, but also recognition of the basic fact that the past informs social conduct and projected futures structure human conduct.

Many laboratory researchers came to accept the methodological dictum that in order to "do science" it was necessary to make the acts of individuals the units of analysis and to treat the acts as objects. It became almost standard procedure for sociological laboratory researchers to create contexts wherein the participants were not allowed to see or hear each other, to deceive the participants, and quantify the responses of individuals to stimuli provided by the researchers. The acceptance of the dictum that the participants could not be allowed to interact "assured that no social processes would be elicited within the laboratory" (Couch, Katovich, and Miller, 1987: 12).

An example of a host of such studies is one completed by Ridgeway, Berger, and Smith (1985). The study purports to examine the relationships between status differences and nonverbal behavior, a reasonable sociological question. A naive subject and shill were convened for each encounter. The participants were seated across a table from each other and separated by an opaque curtain. The shill was instructed that when the curtain opened he was to gaze directly at the subject and not break the gaze until the subject looked away. The subject and shill did not interact; contact was restricted to the shill staring at the subject. No social processes were elicited. The analysis was restricted to noting the response of the naive subject to the staring of the shill. Status rankings had been assigned to the shill by the researchers. Correlations between the assigned status rankings and the rapidity of the naive subject's response of looking away were computed. Such studies fail to elicit even rudimentary social processes. Furthermore, the analyses are limited to noting amount, intensity, and rapidity of the responses of individuals. As Molseed and Maines (1987) note, researchers who complete studies of this type do not contribute to the sociological tradition.

The researchers who undertake such studies seem to be so concerned with the production of discrete individual acts that are easily quantifiable that they fail to recognize that they are not attending to any social phenomena. The activity elicited in these laboratory studies has little, if any, relevance to sociological issues. This type of study has become almost routine for sociologists. The sociological tradition and imagination that informed the early work of Sherif and Lewin and was still a viable part of the research of Swanson (1953) and Rose and Felton (1955) has faded from the scene. Many of these studies are so far removed from sociological concerns that even those conducting them cannot identify the sociological issues addressed (Couch, Katovich and Miller, 1987: 12).

The decline in a concern with sociological issues and the emergence of highly contrived situations that elicit the responses of individuals in the laboratory seems to have been in part a concern with the problem of interobserver reliability. If observers cannot achieve at least a modicum degree of agreement on what they have observed it is, of course, impossible to formulate scientific principles. If the attention of observers is clearly focused on simple responses it is easier for observers to achieve agreement than when attention is focused on complex social phenomena.

The complexity, rapidity and, ever-changing nature of social action provides a severe challenge to students of social processes and group behavior. One technique adopted by many laboratory researchers to achieve an adequate level of interobserver reliability has been to focus attention on the acts of individuals. That approach, of course, does not provide a viable resolution of the problem. Rather, it results in nonsociological research. A more viable procedure for improving interobserver reliability is to record the activity. However, relatively few sociologists have used recording technologies to enhance their observations of activity elicited in the laboratory. The recording of social action does not automatically resolve all the problems associated with observing human conduct. To complete a sociological analysis it is still necessary to make social acts—the activity of dyads, triads, and pentads the focus of attention when analyzing the recordings.

Those sociologists who have attempted to resolve complex problems of observing of human conduct by instituting controls that prohibit laboratory participants from interacting have thereby assured that they will not generate data that are of any utility to the formulation of principles of social life. They have substituted scientism for science. Researchers can make units of social action their focus of attention without using audio-visual recording technologies. However, when researchers make only unaided direct observation of social processes it is very difficult to achieve adequate levels of interobserver agreement for the formulation of principles of social action.

A COUNTER POSITION

Concurrently with the development of measurement procedures that focused attention on individuals the sociological tradition of symbolic interactionism that stems from the writings of Dewey, Cooley and Mead matured. That theoretical tradition explicitly calls for the study of social processes. The founders of the symbolic interaction tradition articulated an ontology that recognized human life rested on a social foundation, was processual, transformed, emerged, and was expressed in many different forms. They alluded to, but did not articulate, the fantastically complex nature of social phenomena. They called for the formulation of abstract principles of social processes, but did not formulate methodological procedures for accomplishing that objective.

More recent advocates of that tradition, particularly Blumer (1969), have formulated in broad outline a methodology that they argued is consistent with the tenets of symbolic interaction theory (Athens, 1984a, 1984b). That methodology is rooted in the ethnographic tradition of Darwin. It calls for entering into naturally occurring social processes to detect how individuals fit together their lines of action to produce social action and to note the consequences of various forms of social action. The methodological procedures offered do not provide data that are sufficiently precise, shareable and researchable to allow for the development of precise and abstract principles of social life (Couch, 1986a).

Furthermore, while the methodological dictums of traditional symbolic interactionists direct attention to social processes, the tradition does not provide an adequate set of concepts for the analysis of social phenomena. Dewey and Mead were far more schooled in psychology than in sociology. They recognized the social foundation of human life, but they did not have command of many sociological concepts. They were for the most part unaware of or indifferent to the sociological concepts of Marx, Simmel, and Durkheim.

Nonetheless, symbolic interactionists have maintained that a science of human behavior can only be developed by the systematic study of social processes, but their insistence upon studying social processes only as they "naturally occur" has inhibited the formulation of general principles of human conduct. As Lofland (1970: 37) has noted, most interactionists have been content to: (1) offer "doctrinaire reiterations of the teachings of the masters," (2) translate the general orientation into statements that "make slightly more specific the general imagery," and (3) the completion of case studies that have an affinity with interaction theory.

That development has been in part a consequence of the general acceptance among interactionists of Blumer's disavowal of control. Blumer (1980) repudiates laboratory procedures on the grounds they are inconsistent with the epistemology implied by interaction theory and that they are artificial. But, laboratory procedures are not inconsistent with the epistemology of Mead (McPhail, 1979; McPhail and Rexroat, 1980a, 1980b; Buban, 1986; Kohout, 1986). Even if the interaction tradition and laboratory procedures were contradictory, such a reason would not be adequate grounds for the dismissal of laboratory procedures if it can be demonstrated that they can generate data that bear upon the questions posed by the theory.

The rejection of laboratory procedures on the grounds of artificiality rests upon the presumption that it is impossible to elicit social phenomena that is isomorphic with the social activity human beings produce in naturally occurring encounters. But, negotiations can be elicited within controlled contexts that are similar to the negotiations that are constructed in the everyday lives of human beings; and, those negotiations, if they are produced in a relatively uncluttered context, can be subjected to far more precise and detailed analysis than can field observations.

Perhaps the major reason interactionists have rejected the laboratory is that they regard laboratory research as necessarily requiring the establishment of, if not a tyrannic relationship between researchers and researched, at least a highly authoritarian relationship. And, most interactionists are committed to egalitarianism. Most are reluctant to institute an asymmetrical relationship between themselves and those they research. It is true that most sociologists who have completed laboratory studies have initiated a highly authoritarian relationship between themselves and their subjects. While few, if any, have established a tyrannic relationship, most laboratory researchers routinely deceive their subjects which is a mild form of tyranny. Most interactionists repudiate such procedures.

How dyads, triads, and larger units create social orders and the consequences of the orders they create can be examined in a laboratory context without deception or the initiation of a tyrannic relationship. Nor need laboratory researchers limit themselves to such questions as: What causes human conduct? Laboratory research can address such issues as how do human beings join together their individual lines of action to create social encounters and social structures. In fact the completion of viable laboratory studies of human conduct is contingent upon the recognition that human beings initiate as well as respond; that they create as well as are created. The controls possible in laboratory studies allows for far more detailed and precise analysis of the emergent qualities of social processes than is possible on the basis of unenhanced naturalistic observations; the controls if properly exercised do not destroy the possibility of studying the emergent qualities of human conduct in the laboratory.

Another factor that appears to fuel the antagonism of symbolic interactionists toward laboratory studies is that they regard laboratory data as having low fidelity; that it does not adequately mirror social action produced in uncontrolled contexts. Of course, in one sense it does not. It does not attempt to reproduce all the complexity of much day-to-day human conduct. Rather, it attempts to simplify select phenomena to render critical features more observable. One way that is achieved is to create impoverished contexts of a particular type so that the social processes of concern are displayed in bold relief. The objective is to reproduce in an uncluttered manner those elements of sociation that constitute forms of social action or social relationship so that they can be more easily detected.

The production of data of high fidelity and the exercise of controls are not inherently incompatible. However, the generation of high fidelity data of social phenomena is contingent upon creating contexts wherein participants are allowed to interact and construct a small social world within circumscribed situations. Furthermore, in order to make high fidelity data available to researchers it is necessary to make a record of the phenomena that retains the events in much the same form as their original form. Audio-visual recording devices allow for that possibility. The events displayed by recordings have far greater isomorphism with the original phenomena than do either human memory enhanced by field notes or questionnaire responses.

A MERGER

Naturalistic field studies and laboratory studies that include the recording of social phenomena are not incompatible. Most of the theortical issues addressed by naturalistic observers can also be addressed in the laboratory. For example, Strauss and his associates have completed a series of studies of negotiation processes (Strauss et al., 1963; Strauss, 1978). The same processes, both interpersonal negotiations (Sink and Couch, 1986) and intergroup negotiations (Weiland, 1977), have also been studied in the laboratory. The former set of studies have powerfully demonstrated that human beings construct social orders in their day-to-day lives as well as adopt to extant social orders. The latter studies have isolated in a fairly precise manner the constituent parts of negotiations, noted the similarities and differences between interpersonal and intergroup negotiations and offer a comprehensive set of concepts for the explication of negotiations.

Both sets of studies apply an informed sociological frame of thought to social phenomena and acknowledge and further demonstrate the processual nature of human life. The studies of Strauss and associates examine how two parties interrelate to modify or construct social orders. The study of Sink and Couch isolated the elements of sociation that compose interpersonal negotiations and demonstrate how individuals construct micro-orders; Weiland's study demonstrates how representatives construct macro-orders through the negotiation of collective differences.

Many different forms of social action and social relationships can be researched both in the field and the laboratory. They range in complexity from the study of interaction between a parent and child when the parent is instructing the child to the complex interrelationships within and between corporate groups.

The formulation of generic propositions by both types of studies will be facilitated if observations from two or more sites are constantly compared (Glaser and Strauss, 1967). Then, if the results of field and laboratory studies are compared, grounded theories of social conduct that have universal applicability can be constructed. Perhaps, in due time such theories will replace the disembodied theories that now pervade much of social science.

The ultimate test of propositions formulated on the basis of laboratory studies is a demonstration that the same order prevails in everyday life. In that sense assertions based upon field observations have greater validity than assertions based on laboratory generated data. However, conversely, laboratory generated data will often lead to the discovery of sequences and structures that are difficult to detect in the field. When that occurs the principles formulated on the basis of laboratory data can then be tested, explicated and extended on the basis of field studies.

The elements and structures of openings to coordinated action were first isolated in the laboratory. Their validity was then demonstrated by field observations that demonstrated that the same elements were produced when people constructed openings in naturally occurring situations (Miller, Hintz, and Couch, 1975). The field observations of naturally occurring openings revealed that more elements of sociation were often produced in openings to coordinated action than had been detected in the laboratory study. The field studies of openings elaborated upon and extended the laboratory findings.

Whereas field studies provide the ultimate tests for and extend laboratory findings, laboratory studies usually allow for the formulation of more precise principles than is possible on the basis of field observations. Generally speaking it simply is not possible to establish precise propositions on the basis of field observations. The ability to demonstrate in detail and with precision the linkages between elements of sociation and their sequential order is one of the outstanding strengths of laboratory studies.

The vitality of the biological sciences has been greatly enhanced by the cross fertilization that has occurred by interfacing ethnographic studies with laboratory studies (Mayr, 1982). The same type of cross fertilization is possible in sociology if laboratory researchers inform themselves about the field studies completed on the issues they are interested in studying and, if field researchers inform themselves about the laboratory studies completed on the issues they are studying.

THE FUTURE

From the beginning of the discipline when Comte coined the term sociology and advocated a science of society, the hope and promise has been that through the systematic examination of social phenomena generic principles of social conduct could be formulated. Some steps toward that hope and promise have been taken. However, a considerable amount of human effort has been essentially wasted. Many of the would be builders of a science of society have been so concerned with achieving recognition from the intellectual community that sociology is truly a science that they have unreflectively imitated what they regard as the procedures of the inorganic sciences. That has enticed many of them to formulate questions and adopt procedures that make it impossible to construct a science of society. Many of them in their concern to be scientific have insistently denied the necessity of adapting their research procedures to the distinctive qualities of human life. Many of these misled souls have refused to recognize that a science of society cannot be constructed within the parameters of the mechanical paradigm.

Human life has dimensions that are not present in inorganic or organic phenomena. A science of society cannot be constructed if sociologists continue to insist that social processes are not distinctively different from inorganic and organic processes. To develop a vibrant social science it will be necessary for sociologists to free themselves from the constraints of the mechanistic paradigm and formulate a new paradigm that recognizes the distinctive qualities of human life (Couch, 1982).

Laboratory studies of social processes as well as other methods can contribute to the objective of establishing a science of society, but only if laboratory researchers design their studies with full recognition that participants in laboratory studies have the same qualities as do those who design the studies. That somewhat complicates the task of laboratory researchers. It requires them to walk the tightrope between exercising control and eliciting select forms of social behavior. However, that tightrope is far easier to walk than many imagine. Control can be achieved by presuming a cooperative relationship between researchers and researched. Subjects ranging from unsophisticated children to Ph.D.s in sociology will usually willingly accept the parameters provided them by researchers. When volunteers enter the laboratory context most of them will with the best of their abilities attempt to organize their actions within the parameters provided by the researchers. That allows researchers to generate relatively uncluttered specimens of social phenomena.

However, to elicit social action it is necessary to allow the participants to project futures and to establish relationships among themselves. To accomplish that, it is necessary to allow participants to exercise their wills, to have some autonomy; they often create unanticipated social objectives and reformulate the parameters provided. That occurs both inside and outside of the laboratory. That, of course, may have the consequence of the participants establishing and acting within contexts other than those desired by the researcher.

For example, in one study of intergroup negotiations the three persons convened to serve as partisan group members decided that neither the position of the opposition nor the one assigned to them had merit. They went further and concluded those who had designed the study did not understand the issues. Consequently, they decided that they would not take part in the farce. They would not suspend their disbelief and use the stage we had provided. The only consequence for the research endeavor was the necessity of running an extra session.

Control, of course, is a necessary ingredient of laboratory studies but if the control is too great it can destroy the phenomena under investigation. Furthermore control is not the only ingredient necessary for the completion of vital laboratory studies of social phenomena. It is also necessary to create a context wherein the participants will act as human beings, not respond as robots to stimuli. Ideally they are provided with an opportunity to strut their stuff. That can best be achieved by using the laboratory as a provocative stage (Katovich, 1985: 60–63). The use of the laboratory as a provocative stage does not necessarily mean that high drama will be produced. In fact, the production of high drama may be counter productive. When high drama is elicited there is a greater likelihood that the participants will violate the parameters provided by the researchers. On the other hand, the production of high drama is necessary if certain questions are to be studied in a laboratory context. That further complicates the tasks of laboratory researchers but it is not an unmanageable problem.

It is not possible to study all social phenomena in the laboratory; nor can all sociological questions be translated into laboratory research problems. It is not possible to recreate German Nazism in the laboratory; nor is it possible to recreate the Senate of the United States in the laboratory. And, these and other social phenomena of the same order are worthy of sociological analyses. However, it is possible to produce highly asymmetrical authority relationships in the laboratory (Milgram, 1968) and elicit obedience; and, it is possible to produce representative relationships (Weiland and Couch, 1986; Couch and Weiland, 1986) and intergroup negotiation between representatives in the laboratory (Weiland, 1977; Couch and Murabito, 1986). The laboratory studies of authority and obedience illuminate the nature of authority relationships and specify some of their consequences. Such studies can and have illuminated some facets of Nazism. In a similar manner studies of the representative relationships and intergroup negotiations illuminate some of the critical dimensions of legislative conduct.

The knowledge obtained from such studies may not only provide greater understanding of these social processes and relationships, but might provide information that will allow human beings to construct more pleasant and satisfactory forms of social action and relationships.

An implicit presumption of the procedures offered in this statement is a clear division of labor between researchers and participants. That is unfortunate. That division, especially as it is reflected in some laboratory studies of human conduct that refers to the researchers with a capital E and the participants with a capital S, is an undesirable heritage. Perhaps such a division was necessary in order for laboratory research of human conduct to become established. However, it seems that social scientists now have sufficient sophistication that at least the hierarchical dimension of that division can be lessened, if not eradicated. A division of labor does not necessarily imply a hierarchy. And, it certainly does not require a closed awareness context wherein one party is kept in the dark about the objectives of the other. If there is merit to the idea of a science of society, it ought to be possible to entice others besides social scientists to contribute to the enterprise without deceiving them. If that is not possible perhaps the sociological enterprise should be abandoned. Nor need the contributions of others be limited to serving as participants (or as some say as S's); they can also actively participate in the analysis and interpretation of the data.

Most of the illustrations offered in this statement concern themselves with how human beings jointly produce various forms of social action and social relationships. The focus of these studies has been to a large extent on what is denoted by the phrase "a science of society." However, the procedures are not limited to such questions. They can, with adaptations, be employed to study such phenomena as culture (Rose and Felton, 1955; McFeat, 1974) and the issues implied by the phrase "the individual and society."

The procedures offered in this statement are not unique. The distinctive feature of this statement is the combination offered. Specifically it calls for a recognition that human life rests upon a foundation of social processes as specified by symbolic interaction theory, that the proper study of human conduct is the study of social processes, and that the study of social processes can be facilitated by the sociologically informed use of the laboratory and audio-visual recordings. If and when that occurs, laboratory research will enrich the sociological tradition and laboratory research will be enriched by the sociological tradition.

Bibliography

Asch, Soloman

1951 "Effects of group pressure upon the modification and distortion of judgement." In H. Guetzkow (ed.), Groups, Leadership and Men. Pittsburg, PA: Carnegie Press.

Athens, Lonnie H.

1984a "Blumer's method of naturalistic inquiry: a critical examination." Pp. 241–258 in Norman K. Denzin (ed.), Studies in Symbolic Interaction, Vol. 5. Greenwich, CT: JAI Press.

1984b "Scientific criteria for evaluating qualitative studies." Pp. 259–268 in Norman K. Denzin (ed.), Studies in Symbolic Interaction, Vol. 5. Greenwich, CT: JAI Press.

Babbie, Earl R.

1973 Survey Research Methods. Belmont, CA: Wadsworth.

Bales, Robert F.

1968 "Interaction process analysis." Pp. 465–471 in D. L. Sills (ed.), International Encyclopedia of the Social Sciences, Vol. 7. New York: Macmillian.

Bales, Robert F.

1950 Interaction Process Analysis. Cambridge, MA: Addison-Wesley.

Becker, Howard S. and Blanch Geer

1957 "Participant observation and interviewing." Human Organization 16 (Fall): 28–32.

Berger, Joseph and Morris Zelditch

1985 Status, Rewards and Influence. San Francisco: Jossey-Bass.

Blalock, Hubert M.

1960 Social Statistics. New York: McGraw-Hill.

Blumer, Herbert

1969 Symbolic Interactionism. Englewood Cliffs, NJ: Prentice-Hall.

1980 "Social behaviorism and symbolic interactionism." American Sociological Review 45: 409–419.

Borgotta, Edgar F.
1981 "The small groups movement: historical notes." American Behavioral Scientist 24: 607–618.
Buban, Steven L.
1976 "Focus control and prominence in triads." Sociometry 39 (September): 281–288.
1986 "Studying social process: the Chicago and Iowa Schools revisited." Pp. 25–38 in Carl J. Couch, Stanley L. Saxton, and Michael A. Katovich (eds.), Studies in Symbolic Interaction: The Iowa School. Greenwich, CT: JAI Press.
Campbell, Donald T. and Julian C. Stanley
1963 Experimental and Quasi-Experimental Designs for Research. Chicago: Rand McNally.
Caplow, Theodore
1968 Two Against One: Coalitions in Triads. Englewood Cliffs, NJ: Prentice-Hall.
Couch, Carl J.
1986a "Questionnaire, naturalistic observation and recordings." Pp. 45–59 in Carl J. Couch, Stanley L. Saxton, and Michael A. Katovich (eds.), Studies in Symbolic Interaction: The Iowa School. Greenwich, CT: JAI Press.
1986b "Elementary forms of social activity." Pp. 113–129 in Carl J. Couch, Stanley L. Saxton, and Michael A. Katovich (eds.), Studies in Symbolic Interaction: The Iowa School. Greenwich, CT: JAI Press.
1984a "Symbolic interaction and generic sociological principles." Symbolic Interaction (Spring): 1–13.
1984b Constructing Civilizations. Greenwich, CT: JAI Press.
1982 "Temporality and paradigms of thought." Pp. 1–24 in Norman K. Denzin (ed.), Studies in Symbolic Interaction, Vol. 4. Greenwich, CT: JAI Press.
1975 "Obdurate features of social life." Pp. 237–254 in Carl J. Couch and Robert A. Hintz, Jr. (eds.), Constructing Social Life. Champaign, IL: Stipes.
Couch, Carl J., Michael A. Katovich, and Dan E. Miller
1987 "The sorrowful tale of small groups research in social psychology." To appear in Norman K. Denzin (ed.), Studies in Symbolic Interaction, Vol. 8. Greenwich, CT: JAI Press.
Couch, Carl J., Stanley L. Saxton, and Michael A. Katovich (eds.)
1986 Studies in Symbolic Interaction: The Iowa School. Greenwich, CT: JAI Press.
Couch, Carl J. and Marion W. Weiland
1986 "A study of the representative-constituent relationship." Pp. 375–Carl J. Couch, Stanley L. Saxton, and Michael A. Katovich (eds.), Studies in Symbolic Interaction: The Iowa School. Greenwich, CT: JAI Press.

Couch, Carl J. and John Murabito
1986 "Mediating intergroup negotiations." Pp. 365–374 in Carl J. Couch, Stanley L. Saxton, and Michael A. Katovich (eds.), Studies in Symbolic Interaction: The Iowa School. Greenwich, CT: JAI Press.

Couch, Carl J., Joel O. Powell and Mari Molseed
1985a The Study of Social Processes I: Design. Iowa City, IA: The University of Iowa Video Center. (A Video Production.)
1985b The Study of Social Processes II: Analysis. Iowa City, IA: The University of Iowa Video Center. (A Video Production).

Couch, Carl J. and Robert A. Hintz, Jr.
1975 Constructing Social Life. Champaign, IL: Stipes Publishing Co.

Cressy, Donald R.
1953 Other People's Money. Glencoe, IL: The Free Press.

Denzin, Norman K.
1978 The Research Act, second edition. New York: McGraw-Hill.
1984 "Retrieving the small social group." Pp. 35–48 in Norman K. Denzin (ed.), Studies in Symbolic Interaction, Vol. 5. Greenwich, CT: JAI Press.

Drabek, Thomas E. and Eugene Hass
1967 "Realism in laboratory simulation: myth or method?" Social Forces 45 (March): 337–346.

Durkheim, Emile
1915 The Elementary Forms of Religious Life. Translated by Joseph Ward Swain. London: Allen and Unwin.

Eisely, Loren
1961 Darwin's Century. Garden City, NY: Doubleday and Co.

Emerson, Joan
1970 "Nothing unusual is happening." Pp. 208–222 in Tomatsu Shibutani (ed.), Human Nature and Collective Behavior: Papers in Honor of Herbert Blumer. Englewood Cliffs, NJ: Prentice-Hall.

Farberman, Harvey A.
1975 "A criminogenic market structure: the automobile industry." Sociological Quarterly 16: 438–457.

Glaser, Barney G. and Anselm L. Strauss
1964 "Awareness context and social interaction." American Sociological Review 29 (October): 669–679.

Glaser, Barney G. and Anselm L. Strauss
1967 The Discovery of Grounded Theory. Chicago: Aldine.

Hall, Peter M. and Dee Ann Spencer-Hall
1982 "The social conditions of the negotiated order." Urban Life 11: 328–349.

Hall, Peter and Mary Jo Neitz
1986 Ethnographic Research and Generic Sociological Principles. Paper delivered at Midwest Sociological Society Meetings.

Hardesty, Monica J.
1986a "Formal analysis of processual data." Pp. 89–105 in Carl J. Couch, Stanley L. Saxton, and Michael A. Katovich (eds.), Studies in Symbolic Interaction: The Iowa School. Greenwich, CT: JAI Press.
1986b "Plans and moods: a study in therapeutic relationships." Pp. 209–230 in Carl J. Couch, Stanley L. Saxton, and Michael A. Katovich (eds.), Studies in Symbolic Interaction: The Iowa School. Greenwich, CT: JAI Press.

Hare, A. Paul
1962 Handbook of Small Group Research. Glenco, IL: Free Press.

Hare, A. Paul, Edgar Borgotta, and Robert F. Bales
1955 Small Groups: Studies in Social Interaction. New York: Alfred Knopf.

Hewitt, John P. and Randall Stokes
1975 "Disclaimers." American Socialogical Review 40 (Febuary):1–11.

Hintz, Robert A., Jr.
1974 Foundations of Social Action. Ph.D. dissertation. Iowa City, IA: The University of Iowa.

Hintz, Robert A., Jr., and Carl J. Couch
1975 "Time, intention and social behavior." Pp. 47–64 in Carl J. Couch and Robert A. Hintz (eds.), Constructing Social Life. Champaign, IL: Stipes.

Innis, Harold Adams
1951 The Bias of Communication. Toronto: University of Toronto Press.

Jefferson, Gail
1972 "Side sequences." Pp. 294–338 in David Sudnow (ed.), Studies in Social Interaction. New York: The Free Press.

Judson, Horace G.
1979 The Eighth Day of Creation. New York: Simon and Schuster.

Katovich, Michael A.
1984 "Symbolic interactionism and experimentation: the laboratory as a provocative stage." Pp. 49–67 in Norman K. Denzin (ed.), Studies in Symbolic Interaction, Vol. 5. Greenwich, CT: JAI Press.
1986 "Temporal stages of situated activity and identity activation." Pp. 329–352 in Carl J. Couch, Stanley L Saxton, and Michael A. Katovich (eds.) Studies in Symbolic Interaction: The Iowa School. Greenwich, CT: JAI Press.

Katovich, Michael A., Stanley L. Saxton, and Joel O. Powell
1986 "Naturalism in the laboratory." Pp. 79–88 in Carl J. Couch, Stanley L. Saxton, and Michael A. Katovich (eds.), Studies in Symbolic Interaction: The Iowa School. Greenwich, CT: JAI Press.

Katovich, Michael A., Marion W. Weiland, and Carl J. Couch
1981 "Access to information and internal structures of partisan groups." The Sociological Quarterly 22: 432–446.

Kohout, Frank J.
1986 "George Herbert Mead and experimental knowledge." Pp. 7–24 in Carl J. Couch, Stanley L. Saxton, and Michael A. Katovich (eds.). Studies in Symbolic Interaction: The Iowa School. Greenwich CT: JAI Press.

Kuhn, Manford H.
1962 "The interviewer and the professional relationship." Pp. 193–206 in Arnold M. Rose (ed.), Human Behavior and Social Processes. Boston: Houghton-Mifflin.

Leichty, Marilyn G.
1986 "Social closings." Pp. 231–248 in Carl J. Couch, Stanley L. Saxton, and Michael A. Katovich (eds.), Studies in Symbolic Interaction: The Iowa School. Greenwich, CT: JAI Press.

Leichty, Marilyn G.
1975 "Sensory modes, social action and the universe of touch." Pp. 65–79 in Carl J. Couch and Robert A. Hintz Jr. (eds.), Constructing Social Life. Champaign, IL: Stipes.

Lennard, Henry L. and Arnold Bernstein
1969 Human Interaction. San Francisco: Jossey-Bass.

Lewin, Kurt, Ronald Lippet, and Ralph K. White
1939 "Patterns of aggressive behavior in experimentally created 'social climates.'" Journal of Social Psychology X: 271–299.

Lofland, John
1976 Doing Social Life. New York: Wiley and Sons.

Lofland, John
1970 "Interactionists' imagery and analytic interruptus." Pp. 35–45 in Tamotsu Shibutani (ed.), Human Nature and Collective Behavior. Englewood Cliffs, NJ: Prentice-Hall.

Lutfiyya, May Nawal and Dan E. Miller
1986 "Disjunctures and the process of interpersonal accounting." Pp. 131–148 in Carl J. Couch, Stanley L. Saxton, and Michael A. Katovich (eds.), Studies in Symbolic Interaction: The Iowa School. Greenwich, CT: JAI Press.

Maines, David R.
1983 "The sand and the castle: remarks concerning G. P. Stone's critique of small group research." In Norman Denzin (ed.), Studies in Symbolic Interaction, Vol. 5. Greenwich, CT: JAI Press.

Maines, David R. and Mari J. Molseed
1986 "The obsessive discoverer's complex and the 'discovery' of growth in sociological theory." American Journal of Sociology 91: 158–164.

Mayr, Ernest
1982 The Growth of Biological Thought. Cambridge, MA: Harvard University Press.

McFeat, Tom
1974 Small-Group Cultures. New York: Pergamon.

McPhail, Clark
1979 "Experimental research is convergent with symbolic interaction." Symbolic Interaction (Spring): 89–94.

McPhail, Clark and Cynthia Rexroat
1979 "Mead vs. Blumer: the divergent methodological perspectives of social behaviorism and symbolic interactionism." American Sociological Review 44: 449–467.

McLuhan, Marshall
1962 The Gutenberg Galaxy. New York: The New American Library.

Mead, George Herbert
1934 Mind, Self and Society. Chicago: University of Chicago Press.
1938 The Philosophy of the Act. Charles W. Morris (ed.). Chicago: University of Chicago Press.

Mead, Margaret and Gregory Bateson
1977 "On the use of the camera in anthropology." Studies in the Anthropology of Visual Communication 3 (Winter): 77–80.

Milgram, Stanley
1968 Obedience. A film.
1963 "Behavior study of obedience." Journal of Abnormal and Social Psychology 76: 371–378.
1965 "Some conditions of obedience and disobedience to authority." Human Relations 18: 57–75.

Miller, Dan E.
1986a "Hypnosis as asymmetric interaction." Pp. 167–194 in Carl J. Couch, Stanley L. Saxton, and Michael A. Katovich (eds.), Studies in Symbolic Interaction: The Iowa School. Greenwich, CT: JAI Press.
1986b "Milgram redux: obedience and disobedience in authority relations." Pp. 77–105 in Norman K. Denzin (ed.), Studies in Symbolic Interaction, Vol. 7. Greenwich, CT: JAI Press.

Miller, Dan E., Robert A. Hintz, Jr., and Carl J. Couch
1975 "The elements and structure of openings." Pp. 1–24 in Carl J. Couch and Robert A. Hintz, Jr. (eds.), Constructing Social Life. Champaign, IL: Stipes Publishing Company.

Miller, Dan E., Marion W. Weiland, and Carl J. Couch
1978 "Tyranny." Pp. 262–288 in Norman K. Denzin (ed.), Studies in Symbolic Interaction, Vol. I. Greenwich, CT: JAI Press.

Mills, C. Wright
1955 The Sociological Imagination. New York: Oxford University Press.

Mills, Theodore M.
1967 The Sociology of Small Groups. Englewood Cliffs, NJ: Prentice-Hall.

Mishler, Elliot and Nancy Waxler
1968 Interaction in Families. New York: John Wiley and Sons.

Miyamoto, S. Frank
1970 "The social act: re-examination of the concept." Pp. 293–300 in Gregory P. Stone and Harvey Farberman (eds.), Social Psychology Through Symbolic Interaction. Waltham, MA: Ginn-Blaisdell.

Molseed, Mari O.
1987 "The form-content bond in the construction and transformation of relationships." To appear in David R. Maines and Carl J. Couch (eds.), Communication and Social Structure. Springfield, IL: Charles C. Thomas.
1986 "Time and form in triadic interaction." Pp. 255–268 in Carl J. Couch, Stanley L. Saxton, and Michael A. Katovich (eds.) Studies in Symbolic Interaction: The Iowa School. Greenwich, CT: JAI Press.

Molseed, Mari O. and David R. Maines
1987 "Sources of imprecision and irrationality in expectation states theory." To appear in Norman K. Denzin (ed.), Studies in Symbolic Interaction Vol. 8. Greenwich, CT: JAI Press.

Neff, Ronald
1975 "Toward an interactionist theory of social structure." Pp. 183–193 in Carl J. Couch and Robert A. Hintz Jr. (eds.) Constructing Social Life. Champaign, IL: Stipes.

Nixon, Howard L.
1979 The Small Group. Englewood Cliffs, NJ: Prentice-Hall.

Orne, Martin T.
1962 "On the social psychology of the psychological experiment: with particular reference to demand characteristics and their implications." American Psychologists 17 (October): 776–783.

O'Toole, Richard and Robert Dubin
1968 "Baby feeding and body sway." Journal of Personality and Social Psychology 10: 59–65.

Powell, Joel O.
1985 "Diffusion and social relations." Pp. 295–308 in Carl J. Couch, Stanley L. Saxton, and Michael A. Katovich (eds.), Studies in Symbolic Interaction: The Iowa School. Greenwich, CT: JAI Press.

Ridgeway, Cecilia L., Joseph Berger, and LeRoy Smith
1985 "Nonverbal cues and status: an expectation states approach." American Journal of Sociology 90: (955–978).

Rose, Edward and William Felton
1955 "Experimental histories of culture." American Sociological Review 20 (August): 383–392.

Saxton, Stanley L.
1973 Reactions to absurd behavior. Ph.D. dissertation. Iowa City, IA: University of Iowa.

Saxton, Stanley L. and Carl J. Couch
1975 "Recording social interaction." Pp. 255–262 in Carl J. Couch and Robert A. Hintz, Jr. (eds.), Constructing Social Life. Champaign, IL: Stipes.

Schegloff, Emanuel A.
1977 "Identification and recognition in interactional openings." Pp. 415–450 in Ithiel de Sola Pool (ed.), The Social Impact of the Telephone. Cambridge, MA: The MIT Press.

Schegloff, Emanuel A.
1968 "Sequencing of conversational openings." American Anthropologist 70: 1075–1095.

Schegloff, Emanuel A. and Harvey Sacks
1973 "Opening up closings." Semotics 8: 290–327.

Schwatz, Howard and Jerry Jacobs
1979 Qualitative Sociology. New York: The Free Press.

Scott, Marvin B. and Stanford M. Lyman
1968 "Accounts." American Sociological Review 33: 46–62.

Sehested, Glenda J.
1975 "The evolution of solidarity." Pp. 99–118 in Carl J. Couch and Robert A. Hintz Jr. (eds.), Constructing Social Life. Champaign, IL: Stipes Publishing Co.
1972 A Laboratory Analysis of Karl Marx on Exploitation, Consensus and Revolution. M.A. thesis. Iowa City, IA: University of Iowa.

Sehested, Glenda J. and Carl J. Couch
1986 "The problem of authoritarianism and laboratory research." Pp. 61–88 in Carl J. Couch, Stanley L. Saxton, and Michael A. Katovich (eds.), Studies in Symbolic Interaction: The Iowa school. Greenwich, CT: JAI Press.

Sherif, Muzafer
1935 "A study of some social factors in perception." Archives of Psychology 27 (No. 187): 1–60.
1936 The Psychology of Social Norms. New York: Harper and Row.

Sica, Alan
1983 "Parsons, Jr." American Journal of Sociology 86: 200–219.

Simmel, Georg
1950 The Sociology of Georg Simmel. Translated and edited by Kurt Wolff. New York: The Free Press.

Sink, Barbara Berger and Carl J. Couch
1986 "The construction of interpersonal negotiations." Pp. 149–166 in Carl J. Couch, Stanley L. Saxton, and Michael A. Katovich (eds.), Studies in Symbolic Interaction: The Iowa School. Greenwich, CT: JAI Press.

Stone, Gregory P.
1962 "Appearance and self." Pp. 86–118 in Arnold M. Rose (ed.), Human Behavior and Social Processes. Boston: Houghton Mifflin.

Strauss, Anselm, L.
1978 Negotiations: Varieties, Contexts, Processes and Social Order. San Francisco: Jossey-Bass.

Strauss, Anselm L., Leonard Schatzman, Donuta Erlich, Rue Bucher, and Melvin Sabshin
1963 "The hospital and its negotiated order." In Eliot Friedson (ed.), The Hospital in Modern Society. New York: The Free Press.

Swanson, Guy
1953 "A preliminary laboratory study of the acting crowd." American Sociological Review 18: 522–543.

Tedeschi, J. T. and M. Reiss
1980 "Verbal strategies in impression management." Pp. 271–302 in C. Antaki (ed.), The Psychology of Ordinary Language Explanations of Social Behavior. London: Academic Press.

Travisano, Richard V.
1975 "Comments on a research paradigm for symbolic interaction." Pp. 272–280 in Carl J. Couch and Robert A. Hintz, Jr. (eds.), Constructing Social Life. Champaign, IL: Stipes Publishing Company.

Traynowics, Laurel
1986 "Establishing intimacy." Pp. 195–208 in Carl J. Couch, Stanley L. Saxton, and Michael A. Katovich (eds.), Studies in Symbolic Interaction: The Iowa School. Greenwich, CT: JAI Press.

Turner, Ralph H.
1953 "The quest for universals in sociological research." American Sociological Review 24 (June): 605–611.

Webb, Eugene J., Donald T. Campbell, Richard D. Schwarts, and Lee Sechrest
1966 Unobtrusive Measures: Nonreactive Research in the Social Sciences. Chicago: Rand McNally.

Weiland, Marion W.
1975 "Forms of social relations." Pp. 80–98 in Carl J. Couch and Robert A. Hintz, Jr. (eds.), Constructing Social Life. Champaign, IL: Stipes Publishing Company.
1977 Representation, Responsibility and Negotiations. Ph.D. dissertation. Iowa City, IA: The University of Iowa.

Weiland, Marion W. and Carl J. Couch
1986 "The disintegration and solidification of newly formed partisan groups." Pp. 309–321 in Carl J. Couch, Stanley L. Saxton, and Michael A. Katovich (eds.), Studies in Symbolic Interaction: The Iowa School. Greenwich, CT: JAI Press.

Wieting, Stephen G.
1977 "Microcultural generations." Unpublished manuscript.

Wolf, A.
1950 A History of Science and Technology, and Philosophy in the 16th and 17th Centuries. London: George Allen and Unwin.

Zerubavel, Eveatar
1980 "If Simmel were a field worker: on formal sociological theory and analytical field research." Symbolic Interaction 3: 25–33.

Zimmerman, Don H. and Candice West
1975 "Sex roles, interruptions and silences in conversation." Pp. 105–129 in B. Thorne and N. Henley (eds.), Language and Sex: Differences and Dominance. Rowley, MN: Newbury House Publishers.

Author Index

Subject Index